NEVER RETIRE

Reinvent Yourself for Life's Second Half

BOB LOUDERMILK

Never Retire
Reinvent Yourself for Life's Second Half

Publisher:
> Second Half Press
> Oklahoma City, OK

For more information visit NeverRetire.life or email bob@ NeverRetire.life.

ISBN 979-8-9997719-0-2 (softcover)
ISBN 979-8-9997719-1-9 (hardcover)
ISBN 979-8-9997719-2-6 (eBook)
ISBN 979-8-9997719-3-3 (audio)

Cover design: G&S Cover Design Studio
Editorial team: Tim Peterson and Cristina Wright
Interior design: eBookBurner Technologies

First printing: 2025
Printed in the United States of America

DEDICATION

Dedicated to the bold souls raising the flag of reinvention, again and again, in every season of life. Your vision and courage to begin anew sets a positive example for future generations. You continue to prove that purpose doesn't retire and that passion doesn't expire. The world is better because you didn't settle. This book is for you—and for all those who dare to boldly dream anew.

CONTENTS

INTRODUCTION

MY STORY

If you're wondering why I decided to write a book about reinvention, purpose, and the second half of life, the truth is that my goal wasn't to become an expert on these topics. Like you, I've simply lived long enough to know that life rarely goes according to plan, and that some of the most important chapters happen after you think you've already written the story.

For much of my career, I was deeply involved in the world of entrepreneurship, investing in real estate and building a business in the trade show and events industry. I had the chance to work with hundreds of clients over the years, helping them grow, adapt, and connect. I learned a lot about people, about opportunity, about what it takes to succeed—and what happens when things don't go as expected.

Somewhere along the way, as the years and experiences piled up, I found myself asking deeper questions: *What now? What's next? Is there something more?*

The first half of life had been about building. But the second half was asking something different of me: not just to build, but to grow in new ways. To rethink, to reshape, to reinvest my energy into something that mattered even more.

That process led me to reinvent myself more than once. It wasn't easy. Reinvention never is. There were doubts, setbacks, moments of real struggle—but also incredible lessons. Lessons that are impossible to learn in a classroom or a seminar. Lessons you earn.

Along the way, I became a student of what it really means to thrive in life's second half—diving deep into research, studying the patterns of those who finished strong, and living out those truths myself. I wasn't satisfied with theories; I wanted something real. Something I could stand on.

This book comes from that place. It's not a list of easy answers. It's a conversation built from experience, from research, from hard-earned lessons, and from a deep belief that the best chapters are still ahead.

I'm not writing from a place of having figured it all out. I'm writing as someone who has walked through the questions, wrestled with the changes, lived through the challenges, and found something worth sharing.

Never Retire is not a traditional retirement guide. It's a reinvention guide—a complete reimagining of what the second half of life can be. And it's different from everything else on the shelf:

- It's not about slowing down—it's about showing up.
- It doesn't just inspire—it activates.
- It offers a roadmap, not just advice.
- It's focused on mindset, not just money.

- It honors your experience and capacity.
- It's grounded in science, driven by story, and fueled by purpose.

Reinvention is less about leaving behind who you've been and more about integrating your lived wisdom in service of where you want to go. It's about building upon every lesson, every failure, and every triumph, repurposing them as fuel for the road ahead.

As you turn these pages, I hope you'll see not just my journey reflected, but your own—the questions, the pivots, the hidden strengths waiting to be unearthed.

Thank you for joining me on this path.

Bob Loudermilk

WHY THIS BOOK &
WHY NOW?

The script for life's second half is crumbling. Retirement, as our culture has known it, no longer offers a reliable or desirable path. And you're not imagining it. The world is shifting beneath our feet.

The old retirement mindset—clocking out, kicking back, and fading into irrelevance—is as outdated as a rotary phone in the age of smartphones. Our society built it for a world that no longer exists—a time when work was grueling, lifespans were shorter, and purpose was tied to a paycheck.

We are standing at the crossroads of cultural, economic, and personal change. The traditional retirement system is straining under the weight of demographic realities. Over 10,000 Baby Boomers turn 65 every day. And the promises of pensions, savings, and government support are not enough to sustain meaningful, purposeful lives.

The old model is broken, and it's past time for a new one. *Never Retire* is the new model. We are being called to rethink not just our timelines, but our very definitions of fulfillment and contribution. And whether you're in your 50s, 60s, 70s—or reigniting at any age—what's ahead of you can be the most vital, vibrant, and fulfilling season of your life.

Never Retire is about reclaiming ownership of your life's story, no matter your age or stage. It's about embracing purpose over passivity, reinvention over resignation, and making an impact over being irrelevant. This is not a denial of aging. It is a defiant celebration of the life that remains ahead.

You hold in your hands not just a book, but a blueprint for the most meaningful chapter of your life.

Welcome to *Never Retire*. Let's get started.

PART I
PERSPECTIVE

How you see your life
determines how you live it.

CHAPTER 1

THE POWER OF A PERSPECTIVE FLIP

"The real voyage of discovery consists not in seeking new landscapes, but in having new eyes."
—Marcel Proust

Turning 50 was the only birthday that ever gave me pause. Not because of any midlife crisis—just that lingering thought planted decades ago, in my teenage brain, when 50 looked like the far side of life. Over the hill and on the decline. You hear that message enough times, and it starts to live somewhere in the back of your mind.

And then suddenly, there it was. My next birthday. The big five-zero! But what happened next was totally unexpected.

Every month, a small group of us volunteered to sing at a local nursing home. It was something I looked forward to—simple, meaningful, and a chance to bring a little joy. One day, shortly before my birthday, I met Sally, a resident who was sitting near the front. She was bright-eyed, witty, and sharp. After our performance, we struck up a conversation. As we talked, she told me her age with a twinkle in her voice, almost as if daring me to be impressed.

Ninety-two! I was blown away. Sally had more spark than all the other residents.

She proceeded to tell me something I have never forgotten: *"I so often wish I could go back to my seventies. That was by far the best decade of my life."*

I stood there stunned. Her seventies? The best decade? Here I was, on the brink of 50, feeling the cultural weight of "getting older"—and this woman was longing for her seventies like they were golden years.

That was the moment for me. The flip that forever changed my perspective on aging. If seventy could be the best decade of someone's life, and I was just turning fifty, then I wasn't beginning a descent downhill. I was just hitting my stride. I wasn't running out of time. I was entering the most meaningful part of the journey.

I walked out of that place feeling younger, more hopeful, and strangely energized. That one conversation flipped my entire outlook on aging.

Another Flip

But the story of my new perspective doesn't end there. A month or two later, I was visiting with a family friend, Donna, who's just a few years ahead of me. I asked her if aging ever bothered her. After a long pause, she answered in a quiet, almost reverential way:

"It used to bother me, but something tragic happened that totally changed my outlook. You see, my younger brother died in a car accident in his thirties. Every

birthday since then, I think how fortunate I am that I have the privilege to turn 50. Or 60. Or whatever birthday it is. I'm still alive. I'm still here. And I am so grateful."

Two women. Two perspective flips. Together, they rewrote how I saw aging and what it means to move forward.

What I experienced wasn't just a mood swing. It was something deeper—a *neural shift.* As I later discovered, neuroscience has a name for this: *cognitive reframing.* It's the ability to reinterpret an event in a way that changes how we feel, think, and even how our body responds.

Studies confirm that it's not the events of our lives that shape us most—it's the stories we tell ourselves about them. And when that story changes, so do we.

A shift in perspective can literally restructure your brain, calm your nervous system, and restore your energy. This isn't just psychology—it's biology. And there's a legendary experiment that proves this better than any motivational quote ever could.

The Backward Time Machine: Dr. Ellen Langer's Landmark Study

In 1979, Harvard psychologist Dr. Ellen Langer conducted a groundbreaking experiment—one so surprising that it remains in scientific circles to this day. She wanted to test the power of perceived age on physical and mental

> "Of all the lives you could have lived, how wonderful and special is it that you get to live this one?"
> —James Clear, *Atomic Habits*

performance. Her question was bold: *What if older adults lived as if they were younger, instead of just reminiscing?*

She gathered a group of men in their late 70s and early 80s and placed them in a carefully recreated 1959 environment—a time capsule of their younger selves. Everything in this retreat center reflected the world as it was two decades earlier: magazines, music, décor, television shows. Even the food and conversation topics were pulled from the 1950s.

However, there was one more twist: the men were instructed not to merely recall what life was like. They were told to act as if they were 20 years younger. No one called them "elderly." No one helped them carry their bags. They were treated like capable, independent, vibrant men, because that's what they were pretending to be.

And then the remarkable happened. After just five days immersed in the environment of their younger selves, the men began to change—not just in attitude, but physically:

- Their posture improved
- Their grip strength increased
- Their memory scores rose
- Many showed better hearing and even modest improvements in vision
- Observers said they looked visibly younger

The study didn't reverse aging, but it revealed a profound truth: when we change our mindset, the body often follows. Dr. Ellen Langer called it a *psychological intervention,* but what she really uncovered was a key to possibility. *How we think about age may be just as important as age itself!*

This wasn't some fringe experiment. It laid the groundwork for decades of research on mindset, health, and longevity. And it confirmed what I'd felt deep inside that day in the care home.

Perspective Changes Everything

How we see things shapes how we feel about them. And how we feel shapes how we live. This is the quiet superpower of perspective. And perspective can be flipped in a moment, when you let go of the cultural script and choose a new lens.

Aging isn't something to resist. It's something to reframe. When you shift your focus from what you're losing to what you're gaining—from youth to wisdom, from speed to depth, from uncertainty to clarity—you don't just add years to your life. You add life to your years. And when you finally flip your perspective, you will no longer view life as a slow fade but as a second wind. You will embrace the fact that your best decades may be ahead, not behind.

You don't need more time. You need a better view.

CHAPTER 2

THE VIEW IS BETTER ABOVE 50

The storm howled across Everest's upper slopes. The temperature had dropped to deadly levels, and the wind was clawing at his tent. The summit was within reach—but the air was thin, the storm unforgiving, and the mountain utterly indifferent to his struggle. Every movement was a decision between life and death. And yet, he kept climbing.

In 1975, Xia Boyu first attempted to summit Mount Everest. He was part of a national Chinese team on an historic expedition. But disaster struck. A brutal storm trapped the team high on the mountain. At 26,000 feet, another climber was in critical condition, freezing, and unable to move. Xia had a choice: protect himself or save a life. In an act of courage and compassion, Xia gave the teammate his sleeping bag. That night, he lost both of his legs to frostbite.

Most would've considered that the end of the story. Not Xia. He spent the next four decades rebuilding his body, his mindset, and his mission. Using state-of-the-art prosthetics, he trained relentlessly, preparing for redemption. He fought and overcame cancer. He failed in four separate attempts to summit Everest—one blocked by an avalanche, another by a massive earthquake. And still he climbed.

Fast forward to May 14, 2018. On his fifth try, Xia stood at 29,032 feet, the highest point on Earth. At nearly 70 years old, a man with no legs had done what few believed possible. From the summit, he looked out over the world. He didn't see loss or limitation. He saw everything! Not just the sweeping panorama of Earth, but the summit of his spirit.

The Above 50 Perspective

I chose the word "above" deliberately and intentionally. Not "over 50"—*above* 50. Ask any climber, pilot, or astronaut: there are some things you can't see until you rise above. In your twenties, thirties, and even forties, you're often in the weeds—striving, proving, comparing, and reacting. But above 50, the fog begins to lift, priorities sharpen, the noise fades, and you start to see the bigger picture. You've climbed high enough to finally understand the purpose behind your ascent.

My research and interviews with numerous people confirmed the same thing: something shifts around age 50. The fog of earlier years—ambition, comparison, insecurity—starts to clear. What matters comes into sharper focus. You begin to care less about what people think and more about what truly counts.

Above 50, you:

- **Filter faster.** You waste less time on people, projects, or pursuits that don't align with your purpose.
- **Savor more deeply.** Ordinary moments take on extraordinary meaning.
- **Embrace your uniqueness.** You've lived enough life to realize that conformity is a prison, and that freedom lies in authenticity.
- **Trust your instincts.** Experience has taught you to recognize red flags and green lights.
- **Turn outward.** You begin to think more about what you can give rather than what you can get. The gravitational pull of significance replaces the thirst for success.

You realize that joy comes not from reaching a destination, but from the climb itself—the daily pursuit of meaning, contribution, and connection. This simple shift in perspective can change the direction of your life entirely. You not only increase your chances of living longer. You live broader, deeper, and bolder.

Over the Hill?

You've heard the expression many times: "Over the hill." Though often said jokingly, it's a quiet cultural script that implies your best years are behind you. That you've peaked and the climb is over. But let's take a moment to examine this outdated paradigm closely.

When a climber reaches the summit, do they say, "Well, it's all downhill from here?" Of course not. They pause and breathe. Then they look around and say, "Look at this view!"

> "Other people retire and play cards. I climb."
> —Xia Boyu, Mount Everest Climber

At lower altitudes, the trail is hard to follow. Life is noisy. You're striving, proving, comparing, reacting. But above 50, the fog begins to lift. Priorities sharpen, noise fades, and clarity emerges. You now understand how the many challenges, heartbreaks, and delays were shaping something inside you. It wasn't just about achieving—it was about awakening.

The Positivity Effect

As we grow older, something remarkable happens—not just emotionally, but neurologically.

Psychologists call it *Socioemotional Selectivity Theory*—the idea that as we become more aware of our limited time, we shift our focus away from distractions and toward what matters most. Our focus is now on emotionally rich experiences, deeper relationships, and lasting meaning.

Flowing from that shift is what scientists refer to as the *Positivity Effect*—a tendency to focus more on the good than the bad, not because life gets easier, but because we become wiser about where to place our attention. Our brains start acting like wisdom filters, discarding the irrelevant, clinging to what matters. We worry less about status and more about impact. Less about being impressive and more about being authentic. We begin to:

- Forgive faster
- Dwell less on what we can't control
- Appreciate ordinary moments more
- Find humor and beauty in places we once overlooked

These aren't just theories. They are invitations to live with intentionality, to see aging as a gift, and to flourish by design, not by default.

The positivity effect doesn't mean you ignore problems. It means you don't get stuck in them. You begin focusing on what builds, what inspires, and what lasts. And the best part? You can nurture this shift intentionally through reflection, gratitude, and conscious focus on meaning-rich activities.

The 50+ Opportunity

This shift into perspective and possibility is not just poetic. It's measurable. The data confirms what many of us intuitively feel: the view improves with age.

Research—including reports from the Stanford Center on Longevity and analyses framed by the Kauffman Foundation—shows a surprising trend: adults over 50 are launching new businesses at nearly double the rate of younger cohorts. In fact, entrepreneurial activity is highest among individuals aged 55–64, outperforming those in their 20s and 30s.

This isn't just a small uptick. It's a seismic shift. As the Milken Institute puts it, *"People in their 50s and 60s launch new businesses at nearly twice the rate of people in their 20s."*

Let's get more specific.

- **Entrepreneurship is thriving after 50**. More than 52% of U.S. business owners are age 55 or older, according to the U.S. Census Bureau and Guidant Financial. These second-half entrepreneurs tend to launch ventures rooted in experience, insight, and purpose—not impulse. In fact, a comprehensive MIT and Northwestern study found that founders in their 50s are 2.2 times more likely to succeed than those in their 30s, especially in high-growth startups. They know what works, and they have the grit and patience to see it through.

- **Career reinvention is surging.** The Bureau of Labor Statistics reports that people in their 50s and 60s are pursuing flexible, purpose-driven work more than ever—especially in consulting, teaching, nonprofit leadership, and creative second acts. This isn't about slowing down. It's about recalibrating—choosing roles that align with values, lifestyle, and the freedom to work on their own terms.

- **Unretirement is reshaping the workforce**. A growing number of older adults are not retiring.

They're "unretiring." According to research from Indeed and AARP, more than 37% of people aged 55+ are working by choice, not necessity. Many return to work with a new mindset: doing what they love, with people they respect, at a pace they enjoy. The result? Greater satisfaction, meaning, and energy than ever before.

- **Lifelong learning is exploding.** Platforms like Coursera, edX, and MasterClass report that 30% or more of their adult learners are over age 50. These learners aren't chasing diplomas. They're feeding their curiosity. They're learning coding, AI, watercolor painting, and leadership. And not because they have to, but because they want to grow. It's proof that reinvention often begins with intellectual hunger.

Together, these numbers paint a vivid picture: Rather than being left behind, you're rising into relevance. Instead of phasing out, you're advancing with wisdom, clarity, and power. The climb isn't over. The air is just clearer now.

Final Words from the Summit

Like Xia Boyu, you've weathered the storms and taken some bruises. You've faced moments when the mountain looked too steep, too cold, too brutal. But you kept going, pressing forward when others paused.

You faced your Everest, whatever it was, and you climbed, again and again. You're now reaching your summit. And the view? It's spectacular! You now see that nothing was wasted. Every struggle shaped you, every setback refined you, and every detour built your strength.

Like Xia Boyu, who kept climbing when others thought he was finished, you will reach heights that only persistence, purpose, and perspective can produce. In an interview with TIME Magazine before he successfully ascended, he stated: "I love the mountain. I will fight for it my entire life."

You're not over the hill. You're above it. You have the perspective that others are still climbing to reach. You have hard-earned wisdom, which is so needed. Take time to pause, take in the view, and appreciate the journey. Because you now understand that the view is better above 50. Not because the mountain got easier, but because you got stronger.

> "Everest, for me, I hate it because it took away my legs. I failed to conquer it four times over the past 40 years. But because of my perseverance and effort, Everest eventually accepted me."
> —Xia Boyu, Chinese climber and double amputee, after summiting Everest at age 69 on his fifth attempt.

CHAPTER 3

THE MYTH OF RETIREMENT: LIES YOU WERE TOLD

Retirement isn't the end of the road.
It's just a wrong turn on the way to purpose.

Years ago, our family took a vacation to the mountains of Colorado and visited one of the most fascinating historical sites I've ever seen: the Cliff Dwellings. Built high into the stone walls of the canyon by the Ancestral Puebloans, also known as cliff dwellers, these ancient homes were carved into the rock face and nestled beneath massive overhangs. These people lived, farmed, raised families, and built community—all while suspended on the sides of cliffs.

The sight is breathtaking. The craftsmanship and courage it took to build and live in such a place are hard to put into words. We walked through the preserved ruins, ducked into stone rooms, and imagined what life must have been like hundreds of years ago. The Pueblo people flourished here for generations—until, suddenly, they left.

Near the end of the tour, our guide addressed the mystery that has puzzled historians and archaeologists for decades: Why did they leave? Some have speculated it was due to drought, food shortages, or invasion. But then he shared something that silenced the debate: a simple insight from a researcher who had deeply studied their traditions and culture: *The reason they left was because it was time to go!*

Sometimes, the reason for change isn't dramatic or obvious. It's not always a crisis. It's a quiet knowing. A profound internal shift that says, "This season is over. It's time for something new."

That's precisely what we're seeing with retirement today. For decades, we built lives around a model that made sense for its time. While growing up, we were handed a life script that sounded something like this: Go to school. Get a good job. Work hard. Save your money. Then one day you can kick back, retire, and enjoy the good life.

This was the destination we were promised. Retirement was the gleaming prize at the end of decades of labor. A pot of gold at the end of the rainbow. But here's the uncomfortable truth: The rainbow was painted by someone else. And the pot of gold? For many, it's turned out to be little more than a rusted bucket of unmet expectations.

Because no one told us the whole story. No one told us that retirement, as a concept, is a relatively recent invention. No one told us it was born not from the wisdom of purposeful living, but from the cold calculations of economics and social policy. No one told us that the promise of retirement—"rest" and "reward"—would too often lead instead to restlessness, regret, and even rapid decline.

The old retirement model, like the cliff dwellings, stands as a monument to a way of life that no longer serves us. It's time to leave behind outdated thinking, rigid age-based timelines, and myths of disengagement and decline. We don't need to abandon our values. We just need to relocate them. We need to build new homes that are meaningful, purposeful, and contribute to the modern world.

And to understand what's next, we need to understand where it all began...

The History You Were Never Taught

For most of human history, retirement was not a goal. It wasn't even an option. The expectation that people should work for a set number of years and then withdraw from life is a modern invention, not an eternal truth. It's a social experiment that made sense in a different time and place. But that time is gone, and that place no longer exists.

Retirement, as we've been sold, is a failed promise. A cultural myth built on outdated assumptions, propped up by systems that no longer work. Clinging to it is keeping millions of people stuck, frustrated, and quietly wondering, "Is this really it?"

If you think retirement is the dream, you've been misled. The truth? The happiest, healthiest, and most fulfilled people don't retire. They reinvent, which prepares them for a brighter future. But in order to understand where we're going, we need to first examine how we got here.

The Forgotten Origins: How Retirement Was Invented

For centuries, people didn't retire. They transitioned into a new phase of life. Farmers, artisans, spiritual leaders, and elders stayed active in their communities as long as they could. There was no concept of stepping aside at a certain age. On the contrary, age brought honor and wisdom weight.

The idea that people should stop working at a certain age would have seemed bizarre to these societies. Work wasn't about making a paycheck until an expiration date. It was about contributing to the community for as long as they could because their work was part of who they were.

The modern idea of retirement didn't begin with compassion. It began with strategy. In 1889, German Chancellor Otto von Bismarck introduced the world's first national pension system. It promised financial support to workers over 70, but its motives were not selfless.

Here's the reality behind the policy:

- The average life expectancy in Germany at the time was around 45 years.
- Most people would never live long enough to collect benefits.
- The program created the appearance of support without requiring widespread payouts.

It was a brilliant political move. It appeased growing socialist unrest, boosted the government's image, and encouraged older, less productive workers to exit the workforce—making way for younger, more efficient labor. Retirement wasn't a reward. It was a tool of social engineering.

How Retirement Took Hold in America

The roots of retirement in the U.S. grew out of industrial pressure, not personal fulfillment.

In the 19th century, the Industrial Revolution shifted labor from farms to factories. Work became more physical, time-regulated, and demanding. Older workers, who once passed down skills and wisdom, now struggled to keep pace with long hours and mechanized systems.

By the early 20th century, business owners began quietly pushing out older workers to make room for younger, faster labor. This created a growing dilemma: What should society do with an aging workforce that could no longer meet the demands of industrial jobs, but still needed to survive?

Then came the Great Depression. By 1935, jobs were scarce, and desperation was rising. Young workers needed opportunities. Older workers, with no safety net, were clinging to jobs out of necessity.

Enter President Franklin D. Roosevelt and the Social Security Act of 1935, which formally introduced the retirement age of 65. But that number wasn't based on science or compassion. It was calculated.

- At the time, the average life expectancy for Americans was about 61 years.
- Meaning: most people would never reach retirement age.
- It was a clever fiscal compromise: appear generous, spend less.

Even the early language of Social Security referred to it as "old-age insurance." It was never framed as a reward. It was designed as a safety net—a bare minimum solution for those unable to continue working.

As life expectancies increased and pension programs expanded, the idea became more common that individuals would retire at 65 and spend decades in leisure. A new dream was born—the dream of retirement.

Why It Made Sense Then—But Doesn't Now

In the 1950s and 60s, the idea of retirement took off like wildfire. Employers began offering pensions. Advertising campaigns sold visions of palm trees and golf courses. Retirement communities flourished. And the cultural script became clear: work hard, save enough, and someday you get to stop.

But that story was built on conditions that no longer exist:

- Lifespans were shorter. Most people didn't live into their 80s and 90s.
- Healthcare costs were lower, and employer pensions were generous.
- Fewer people lived with chronic illness, and the pace of life was less demanding.

Today, all of that has changed:

- People are living 20 to 30 years past retirement age.
- Employer pensions have vanished.
- Healthcare and inflation are outpacing savings.
- The average person hasn't saved nearly enough to fund a multidecade retirement. The U.S. median retirement savings for Baby Boomers sits at about $202,000, and nearly 43% of individuals aged 55–64 have no retirement savings at all.

The Hidden Cost of the Retirement Myth

Retirement doesn't deliver on its promise. Instead of being a reward, it often becomes a sentence of boredom, isolation, and aimlessness. Many retirees report feeling lost, irrelevant, and disconnected just a few years in. The thing they longed for becomes a slow fade from purpose.

Let's call it what it is: a well-meaning lie that no longer works.

- It makes people obsolete. The moment you retire, society stops expecting anything of you. You're no longer asked for your wisdom or contribution.
- It accelerates decline. Research shows that retirees experience faster physical and cognitive decline than their working peers.
- It creates financial stress. We've told people to save enough to stop working for 30 years, when most haven't even saved enough for ten.
- It underestimates the human need for purpose. Leisure is lovely, but it was never meant to be a lifestyle.

The Better Way: Reinvention

We don't need a better retirement plan. We need to eliminate the idea of passive retirement altogether! It is a broken idea, a social invention, and it's time to reinvent it again.

What replaces it? A life of continuous reinvention. The most fulfilled people aren't coasting on the sidelines; they're learning, creating, mentoring, exploring, and contributing.

Work isn't something to escape. It's something to evolve. The new model isn't about quitting; it's about shifting. You don't have to work a job you hate forever, but you do need to stay engaged, relevant, and growing.

The people who thrive in the second half of life are those who:

- Shift, not stop. They find new ways to contribute that match their values and energy.
- Stay engaged. Whether it's mentoring, creating, teaching, building, or serving, they continue to grow.
- Live with a mission. They know that the greatest peace doesn't come from withdrawal. It comes from purpose.

Much like the cliff dwellers, we too are standing at the edge of a new frontier. They didn't leave their homes because of a disaster. They left because the season had shifted. They sensed, with quiet wisdom, that it was time to move on. And so must we.

The traditional retirement structure has served its purpose. It stood high and proud for a generation, but it's now hollow. It no longer shelters, inspires, or sustains. It's time to climb down, to look ahead, and to build again—this time not in retreat, but in purpose. Not out of fear, but out of vision. Because the most powerful life is not the one you exit from, but the one you step into with boldness.

CHAPTER 4

BURN THE OLD MAP— REINVENTION STARTS HERE

You don't need a better map.
You need a bolder destination.

The Fire That Changed Everything

In 1988, Yellowstone National Park—one of the most beloved natural treasures in America—caught fire. Small fires, sparked by lightning, flickered across the landscape. At first, they seemed harmless. After all, fires had always been part of Yellowstone's natural cycle. But that summer, something was different. A severe drought gripped the region. Temperatures soared, and wind gusts swept across the mountains, turning sparks into infernos.

What began as a typical summer ignited into what many labeled a catastrophe. Columns of smoke billowed into the sky as flames devoured ancient trees. Visitors were evacuated, and headlines cried out in horror: "Yellowstone Is Burning!"

A staggering 25,000 firefighters battled the flames, but the fires ultimately scorched over a third of Yellowstone's 2 million acres. Flames burned much of America's first national park beyond recognition. Rangers admitted they had never seen anything like it in their lifetimes.

But if you asked Yellowstone itself? It had seen this before—a century earlier, in the massive fires of the 1800s. This kind of event happens roughly every hundred years.

Nature never panicked because it had a secret. Beneath the flames, something remarkable was taking place. This fire, devastating as it appeared, was not the end of the story. It was the beginning of a new one. Yellowstone wasn't dying...it was resetting.

The Lodgepole Pine's Secret

One of Yellowstone's most common trees is the lodgepole pine. If you walked the trails after the fire, you might've thought every single one of them had died. But these trees were waiting.

You see, lodgepole pines produce special cones—serotinous cones—that are sealed shut with a resin so strong, they won't open unless exposed to extreme heat. Ordinary weather can't break them, and time can't crack them. But extreme heat can.

When the fires of 1988 surged through the forests, they did more than destroy. They activated. The cones suddenly opened, and like popcorn, millions of seeds were released. They rained down on a landscape that had been cleared of clutter, flooded with light, and fertilized by ash. The very trauma of the fire had created the perfect conditions for rebirth.

Today, if you visit Yellowstone, you'll see vast forests of trees that were born because of the fire. Because of it, not despite it.

Fire Is Not the Enemy

Contrary to what many assume, periodic fires are necessary for Yellowstone's health. Experts now know that many ecosystems need fire to thrive. Fires remove disease, thin overcrowded trees, return nutrients to the soil, and stimulate the growth of new vegetation.

Forests that never burn? They stagnate, decay, and weaken.

Reinvention Requires a Burn

What if the most painful, disruptive moments in your life weren't signs of failure, but the very heat required to release the seeds of your next chapter? What if retirement—the ending of a career, a role, a season—isn't a death to avoid, but a fire to embrace?

You were not made to wither away in the ashes of what used to be. You were made to regenerate. To reinvent. To grow again—stronger, wiser, and more vibrant than before.

The *Never Retire* mindset doesn't just resist decline. It refuses stagnation. It understands that every forest must burn, and every soul must be reawakened.

The Fire in You

Ask yourself:

- What parts of your life are overgrown and overdue for a burn?
- What clutter is choking the sunlight from your potential?
- What unfulfilled dreams lie dormant, waiting for the heat to wake them?

You may feel like you're being burned. But what if you're being freed?

The Meaning of Reinvention

Reinvention isn't about changing who you are. It's about becoming who you were meant to be all along but perhaps hadn't yet discovered. Like the seeds hidden in those pinecones, the best of you may not have had the right conditions to emerge.

Reinvention is:

- Letting go of old roles that no longer serve you
- Embracing the unknown with courage instead of fear
- Rediscovering your voice, your value, your vitality
- Saying yes to growth even when it's uncomfortable
- Turning pain into power, ashes into opportunity

Why It's Needed Now More Than Ever

The old model of retirement tells people to slow down, fade out, and let go. But we were never meant to retire from purpose.

Today's world needs the wisdom, creativity, and resilience of those in the second half of life more than ever. Companies are starting to realize this. Communities benefit from it, and families are shaped by it. And YOU are ignited by it. Because the truth is: You're not done. You're just different. And the next version of you might be the most powerful one yet.

Pamela Lutrell: Rediscovering Identity After the Nest Empties

Pamela Lutrell had raised three kids and poured herself into her family. She built a reputation as a beloved journalism teacher in San Antonio, Texas. For decades, her days were full, her calendar was booked, and her sense of purpose was clear. But then, the house emptied. When her youngest child moved out, the house became strangely quiet, and daily demands faded. In that silence, something stirred: *Who am I now?*

Pamela had always told herself that one day, when things slowed down, she would finally have "me time." But when that time arrived, it didn't feel like freedom. She had spent years showing up for others. Now she wasn't sure how to show up for herself.

Then came a moment she still remembers with clarity. She renewed her driver's license at age 50. When the new ID arrived in the mail, she looked at the photo and didn't recognize the woman staring back at her. Where was the spark and the vibrancy? The woman in the picture looked tired, faded, and forgotten.

That moment became a mirror. And the mirror became a turning point. Pamela began to change—slowly, gently. She resumed brisk walks and improved her diet. She carved out time to rediscover what brought her joy: writing, fashion, encouragement, and helping other women feel seen and confident.

Then she did something bold. She launched a blog, calling it *Over 50 Feeling 40*—a title that playfully pushed back on society's assumptions. Initially, it was simply a creative outlet. But soon, women began finding her. Women who were asking the same questions and who were also looking for "what's next."

Today, *Over 50 Feeling 40* is followed by thousands of women worldwide. Pamela is now a voice of encouragement and empowerment for those navigating the second half of life. Through speaking, writing, and building community, she's living with more purpose than ever, not because someone gave it to her, but because she followed the ache and turned it into action.

Pamela followed the same roadmap you're now holding. Her story serves as evidence that it's not too late, you're not too ordinary, and you're not disqualified by your age, your past, or your resume.

How to Begin Your Reinvention

Just like Yellowstone, the process begins with a burn, then moves toward intentional growth. Here's how:

1. **Name the Fire.** Identify what's ending or has already ended—career, role, routine, belief system. Name it, grieve it, honor it… Then let it go.
2. **Clear the Ground.** Remove what no longer brings life—habits, relationships, environments, mindsets. Create room for light to reach your core.
3. **Listen for the Seed.** Ask: *What have I always wanted to do? Who do I want to help? What still makes me come alive?*
4. **Plant and Protect.** Take one small step toward that vision—write the book, volunteer, start a project, or learn a new skill. Then guard it from the weeds of doubt.
5. **Let the New You Grow.** Stay consistent and stay rooted. Don't be discouraged by slow progress. Remember: forests don't grow in a week, but they grow stronger because of the fire.

Your Fire Is Your Fuel

In the aftermath of Yellowstone's great fire, one visitor remarked: "It looks dead." But a park ranger smiled and said, "Look closer. It's just beginning."

That's you! You are not a relic of the past. You are a seed of the future. And maybe this fire isn't here to destroy you after all. It's here to release you. Let it burn. Then rise.

CHAPTER 5

REINVENTION BY DESIGN: YOUR PERSONAL BLUEPRINT

"The best way to predict your future is to design it."
—Buckminster Fuller

The Smoke Has Cleared—Now What?

After the flames of Yellowstone died down, something astonishing happened. Scientists and park rangers didn't rush in with bulldozers or blueprints. They didn't try to replant the forest in neat rows or restore it to its original state. Instead, they studied. They observed. They learned what the ecosystem wanted to become, not what outsiders thought it should be.

They worked with nature, not against it. And because of that, Yellowstone didn't just grow back—it grew back better. The fire wasn't a pause. It was a pivot, and the old gave way to the new. Nature didn't wait around wondering what to do next. It began rebuilding immediately, not with panic, but with purpose.

So now it's your turn. So far in this book, we've deconstructed the outdated model of retirement. Struggle, disruption, and "fire" can be the very things that liberate you. You now stand in the "clearing." The map you used to follow is gone, and it's time to do more than rebuild. It's time to design the new you.

Be aware that this is not a cosmetic makeover. It's not about dyeing your hair or learning how to use a new app. Redefining yourself starts with identity and purpose.

Most people quit planning their lives after turning 50. They coast, downshift, and resign themselves to the patterns they already know. But not you. You're reading this because something inside of you is still curious, still eager, still in motion. That's not a leftover spark. It's the start of a second fire.

Reinvention Is Intentional

People don't drift into greatness. They design it. The world may try to define you by your past job, your age, or what you used to be good at. But reinvention isn't about polishing your resume or tweaking your LinkedIn bio. It's about answering a deeper question: What kind of person am I becoming?

The "new you" doesn't emerge by accident. It is a deliberate act of creation. You are the designer. And your life is the masterpiece.

The Science of Reinvention

Neuroscience used to tell us that our brains were mostly fixed after adolescence. But today we know better. Your brain is capable of neuroplasticity—the ability to change and rewire itself—well into your 70s, 80s, and beyond. In fact, learning something new in later life doesn't just help you adapt. It enables you to thrive.

A growing body of research shows that older adults who challenge themselves with new experiences—like learning a new instrument, exploring art, or diving into unfamiliar subjects—report higher levels of life satisfaction, greater mental clarity, and lower rates of depression.

One *PLOS One* study of more than 1,200 adults found that curiosity accelerates after midlife. And this type of engagement boosts emotional vitality, cognitive flexibility, and memory resilience. These findings echo the principles of *Activity Theory*, which holds that staying intellectually and socially active in later life is a key ingredient to flourishing.

Reinvention isn't rebellion. It's renewal, backed by biology. So now that science gives us permission, let's build the new blueprint. Keep in mind that these aren't just steps. They're tools to reignite your identity, using the full power of your past while reaching boldly into your future.

7 Steps to Design the New You

Step 1: Clarify Your Core

Before you build anything new, you must first know what to keep. What are your values—the non-negotiables that define who you are at the root? What do you believe deeply, even when no one else is watching? What has proven true through hardship, success, change, and time?

Think of these as your foundation stones. Even after Yellowstone's fires, the soil remained rich. Not everything had been lost—only what needed to go. In your life, the fire may have cleared out some roles, routines, or relationships. But what's left is often what's most important.

This is where you begin—not with the new, but with the real. Before you try to chase the next chapter, ask, "Who have I always been beneath the titles and tasks?"

One way to clarify your core is to list your five most important values. Then reflect on how those values might be expressed differently, or more fully, in this new season of life. For example, if one of your values is "generosity," maybe now is the time to mentor someone. If it's "excellence," perhaps it's time to finish that book, teach that skill, or explore a craft to master. You don't need to become someone new. You need to become someone true.

Step 2: Reimagine the Canvas

Once you know your foundation, the next step is to dream forward, not backward. Most people think reinvention is about going back to who they used to be or trying to reclaim something they lost. But the real opportunity is to reimagine what life could look like now, based on what matters most to you today.

This isn't a reboot. It's a redesign. So, imagine your life as a blank canvas. If nothing held you back—no fear, no guilt—what would you paint? What colors would dominate your days? What would be at the center of your story?

It could be creativity that never had space to breathe in your earlier years. It could be adventure or peace. Or contributing to a field you admire. Maybe it's starting something small that feels big to you—a podcast, a community group, a side business, or a garden that brings people together.

Take a few minutes to visualize one ideal day. From the first moment you wake up to the moment you go to sleep, what fills your time? Who's around you? What are you doing and what are you feeling? That image is more than just a fantasy. It's a clue. So let yourself dream again.

Step 3: Use What You've Got
Here's a truth we often overlook: Reinvention doesn't start from scratch. It begins from strength.

You've lived, and you've learned. You've built things and you've overcome things. And all of that is raw material for what comes next.

The problem is, we don't always see our value clearly. We downplay what we've done because we compare it to someone else's highlight reel. But take a closer look: you've developed tools over the years—skills, insights, perspectives, instincts—that others don't have. Maybe you led a team. Or managed a household. Perhaps you've served others with compassion or solved problems under pressure. Each experience has weight.

Perhaps you were a manager in operations, and now you can help a local nonprofit organize its supply chain. Maybe you were a parent who learned the hard way how to encourage children, and now you're uniquely positioned to mentor or coach others. Your experiences, even your failures, are not wasted. They are resources.

Try writing down a few of your past roles, whether formal or informal. Under each, jot down what you learned, what you became good at, and what you enjoyed. You'll start to see a pattern. And in that pattern, you'll see the scaffolding for the new you.

Step 4: Start Small, Dream Big

You don't need a five-year plan to start. You need a five-minute window. Most people stall out because they think reinvention needs to be a grand production. They wait for the right time, the perfect strategy, the ideal opportunity. And in the meantime? Nothing changes.

But reinvention doesn't begin with a trumpet blast. It starts with a tiny step. Action changes emotion. Behavior shapes belief. When you move, your identity begins to shift in real time.

So, what can you do today? Maybe it's attending a free event on a topic that interests you. Maybe it's watching one TED Talk or reaching out to someone doing what you want to do. Maybe it's writing one paragraph of that book. Or signing up for a class. Or buying the musical instrument and learning to play it. The point isn't to conquer the mountain. The point is to take the first step up the trail.

Dream as big as you want but act as small as you need to.

Step 5: Design for Vitality, Not Just Activity

It's easy to stay busy. What's harder is staying alive on the inside. In your new design, don't aim for a full calendar. Aim for a full heart.

Reflect on what activities or interactions increase your energy and which ones decrease it. Consider who contributes positively to your conversations and who does not. Use this information to organize your life accordingly.

This is where the Never Retire Equation™ comes in: Calling + Connections + Clues = Alignment.

The Never Retire Equation™—which you'll learn about in a later chapter—states that you need something meaningful to work on (calling), people to share it with (connections), and daily rhythms that support your growth (clues). Even small rituals—such as morning walks, reading time, or weekly coffee with a friend—can make a significant difference.

Look at your week like a designer. Color-code it. What's life-giving? What's dead weight? Then adjust. Not flawlessly, but with intention. Because the goal isn't just to do more, it's to live better.

Step 6: Embrace the Discomfort Zone

There's no such thing as painless growth. To become someone new, embrace being a beginner again. That means stepping into the unknown, trying things that might not work, and giving yourself grace along the way. It means being willing to fail. To look silly and then stumble forward. But it also means feeling alive again.

One woman signed up for a beginner's painting class at 65. She hadn't painted since childhood. The first few weeks were humbling. She struggled to get the colors right, her hands felt clumsy, and she almost quit. But by week six, she realized she didn't just like painting. She absolutely loved it. She had rediscovered a joy that had been buried for decades.

Your reinvention zone will often overlap with your discomfort zone. That's where magic happens. You don't need to be fearless, just willing.

Step 7: Reevaluate Often
Design is not a one-and-done decision. It's a living process and a rhythm. That means pausing every few months. Reflect. Ask yourself:

- Am I growing?
- Am I still aligned with my values?
- Am I becoming someone I admire?

If the answer is yes, keep going. If it's no, adjust. The key isn't speed, but honesty.

You are now the architect of your reinvention, and great architects walk the site often. They refine the design. They notice what's working and what needs to shift. Give yourself that permission. After all, this is your life, so build it well.

A New Version of Yourself May Be Needed

Yellowstone didn't go back to how it was. It became something more powerful. The same is happening for you. So don't settle for what's predictable, and don't shrink to fit your past. Don't fade because the world says it's time to slow down.

The fire made room, and the soil is rich. The canvas is blank, and the brush is in your hand. Begin now designing the new you.

✎ Activation Spotlight

Oklahoma City: From Parking Garage to Global Stage

How Four Questions Can Spark Your Reinvention

You don't need a million-dollar plan to move forward. You just need motion. That truth was demonstrated in 1993 in a city facing hardship.

Oklahoma City was facing a decade of stagnation. Oil prices had collapsed, and they had not yet recovered from an earlier banking collapse. The Medallion was the only hotel downtown, and it rarely had more than a handful of guests at a time. At night, downtown streets were too deserted and dangerous for a guest to venture out to find the one or two restaurants that might be open.

But in a bunker located in a parking garage, a small group of civic leaders met to ask four simple, world-shifting questions:

1. **What could we do?**
2. **What should we do?**
3. **What will we do?**
4. **What's our 30/30?** *(Look back 30 days to reflect. Look forward 30 days to commit.)*

These questions formed the foundation of a bold approach and a new book, *Strategic Doing*.

Pioneered by innovation expert Ed Morrison, *Strategic Doing* works not through elaborate planning, but by creating momentum. This powerful framework is now utilized by communities, universities, and organizations worldwide. But back then, it was just an act of hope in a city on the verge of giving up.

That small group's questions gave rise to *MAPS*—the Metropolitan Area Projects initiative—a time-limited one-cent sales tax designed to fund civic revival in Oklahoma City.

Skeptics said it would never work. Voters disagreed, and the tiny ripple became a tidal wave.

- The MAPS program provided the vision and funding for Chickasaw Bricktown Ballpark, major park upgrades, and a new convention center.
- A new arena was built, attracting an NBA team—the Oklahoma City Thunder (2025 NBA Champions).
- A dead downtown was transformed into a thriving entertainment district, which included the Bricktown Canal and a streetcar system.
- Follow-up initiatives included the building of wellness centers, riverfront trails, boathouses, and the expansion of public art, housing, and social services.

- In 2023, voters approved a $900 million new arena to keep the Thunder in Oklahoma City through 2050, reinforcing the city's growing status as a world-class destination.

And here's the latest: Oklahoma City is confirmed as a location for the 2028 Los Angeles Olympics (LA28), both for softball and the canoe slalom and kayak events.

Strategic Doing for Your Second Half

How does a forgotten city become a world stage for Olympic events and the home of an NBA Championship team? And how does a group of everyday citizens in a parking garage change a skyline, a reputation, and rewrite their city's future? Not with fanfare. Not with a five-year plan. With vision, anchored by action.

When you enter the second half of life, vision becomes even more essential. It's not just about where you've been. It's about what's still possible. And even more: what's still waiting for you?

If a city can reinvent itself and step onto the global stage, what might happen if you asked the same four questions?

➤ What could you do?
Let your imagination off the leash. List the dreams you've shelved. Write down ideas without judgment. What's stirring under the surface?

➤ What should you do?
What aligns with your purpose, this season of life, and what matters most? Which idea stirs something in you? Not everything fits this moment. Choose what makes your heart beat faster.

➤ What will you do?
Pick one thing. Start it within 7 days. Don't wait to feel ready. Act your way into clarity. Clarity comes through motion.

➤ What's your 30/30?
Build in a rhythm of reflection. Every 30 days:

- Look back—What did you try? What did you learn?
- Look forward—What will you commit to next?

PART II
PURPOSE

Energy follows action—and your brain, body, and future are wired for renewal.

CHAPTER 6

THE UNRETIRE ROADMAP: FROM PAUSE TO PURPOSE

"In life, you get to choose: You can make things happen, watch things happen, or stand on the sidelines wondering what just happened. The difference? One lives with purpose. The others just exist."
—Bob Loudermilk

The waves were brutal, and the currents kept dragging her off course. Saltwater stung her lips, and her entire body was battered and raw. But Diana Nyad, at 64 years old, kept swimming—through pain, storms, jellyfish stings, and exhaustion.

She had tried to cross this same stretch of water from Cuba to Florida four times before, but each time she failed. Most would have given up, but Diana wasn't chasing a trophy. She was chasing completion, not with the ocean, but within herself.

Diana grew up in Fort Lauderdale, Florida. At the age of nine, she asked her mother a question while standing on the shoreline: "Where is Cuba?" Her mother pointed out across the sea and said something Diana would never forget. "It's right out there. You, little swimmer, could swim there; it's that close."

That moment planted a dream in Diana's heart. She went on to become a world-class long-distance swimmer in the 1970s, breaking records and making headlines. As life moved on, so did she, transitioning into sports commentary, motivational speaking, and eventually retirement.

But Diana, now in her sixties, began to feel what many do in the second half of life: a longing to reawaken her purpose. She couldn't shake the sense that her most meaningful moment was still out there in the water, unfinished.

At an age when many slow down, Diana chose to speed up. The Cuban swim had become an obsession, despite the numerous obstacles to crossing. First, there's the sheer distance, over 100 miles in the open ocean. Add in crossing a powerful Gulf Stream current and the swirling countercurrents that can easily take a swimmer under. Then factor in other dangers, like sharks, and you'll know why this feat has been called "The Mount Everest of Swims."

Despite the obstacles, in her final attempt—the fifth and successful one—she swam for 53 hours straight, through lightning, nausea, and hallucinations, with no shark cage for protection. When she finally staggered onto the shore in Key West, Florida, completing the 110-mile swim from Cuba, she collapsed into the arms of her team and delivered a short, breathless message to the world:

"Never, ever give up. You're never too old to chase your dreams. And it looks like a solitary sport, but it's a team."

Nyad didn't just finish a swim. She rewrote the narrative of what's possible in the second half of life. She re-entered the arena when most would've stayed on the sidelines. And her story speaks to something deep in all of us: There's still more in you!

You may not swim oceans, but you probably know what it feels like to wonder: "Is this it?" Maybe you retired with good intentions. A chance to slow down, recharge, maybe travel a bit. But something inside you isn't slowing down. Instead, it's stirring, tugging, and whispering to your heart: "You weren't made to retire from meaning. You were made to evolve into a new mission."

Unretirement: The New Revolution

A powerful trend is unfolding worldwide. Increasingly, people who have "retired" are choosing to step back into meaningful work and contribution. And it's not driven by necessity alone. It's driven by desire.

Consider the facts:

- **Labor force participation among Americans aged 65–74 is increasing** and projected to reach 29.8% by 2031. This is up from roughly 26.6% in 2022—the highest level on record.
- **Nearly 40% of retirees later return to work.** Studies based on RAND's Health and Retirement Survey show that, depending on measurement criteria, 26–40% of retirees eventually "unretire" and re-enter the workforce within six years.

- **Almost half would consider returning.** And not just for income, but for connection and purpose. Among Americans aged 50+, about 46% say they'd consider working again if a compelling opportunity emerged. Those with higher education report even higher interest. The motive is often social engagement, purpose, and identity—far more than necessity.

The message is clear: If you're ready to unretire, it begins not with a new job but with a new mindset. Retirement is no longer the final chapter of life. It's an intermission, and the next act is often the most exciting of all. This is the heartbeat of the *Never Retire* philosophy.

The Unretire Roadmap™

> "Whatever your Other Shore is, whatever you must do, whatever inspires you, you will find a way to get there."
> —Diana Nyad, Champion Swimmer

You move through predictable phases in the second half of life, unless you get stuck. This 5-phase model specifically supports people like you—those who refuse to drift or remain stuck. And people who feel the pull toward something more.

The Unretire Roadmap™ will guide you in answering the question, *What now, and how do I begin again?* Each phase of this journey is deeply personal, and you'll probably recognize parts of yourself in each one.

1. The Discomfort Phase (from settling to stirring)
Something just doesn't feel right anymore

Emotional Signals: Restlessness. Frustration. Apathy. Boredom. Confusion.
Behavioral Signs: Coasting. Overcommitment. Escapism. "Numbing out."

You feel it before you can name it. A subtle ache, a longing for more, or just the sense that something is off. You wake up, go through the motions, and maybe even succeed at what you're doing. Yet something in your soul keeps whispering: "This isn't it anymore."

In psychology, this experience is best described through *Self Discrepancy Theory*. It occurs when there's a meaningful gap between your current identity ("actual self") and your deeper sense of who you want to be—your "ideal self" and what you feel you ought to be.

Research shows these discrepancies commonly trigger a life reassessment in midlife and later life—especially during major transitions such as retirement, an empty nest, health changes, or loss of roles like career or caregiving.

This internal misalignment is not a crisis. It's a signpost. It's the mind's way of saying, "Something needs to shift." It's often the beginning of reinvention, renewed purpose, and deeper alignment between identity and action. Don't silence the ache. It's your invitation to a deeper life.

Key Question: *What part of my life no longer fits who I'm becoming?*

2. The Reflection Phase (from noise to clarity)
What do I really want this next chapter to feel like?

Emotional Signals: Ambivalence. Hope. Fear. Curiosity.
Behavioral Signs: Journaling. Daydreaming. Reading. Starting conversations. Revisiting passions.

This is the moment you step away from the noise and start asking bigger questions. During this phase, you may find yourself revisiting childhood dreams or taking long walks with no agenda. Some may even experience crying occasionally without knowing why.

You're making space for the unfinished dream that still stirs inside. And in a world that worships hustle, reflection is an act of courage. It might feel strange or even scary, but stay with it. You are peeling away the false layers to rediscover what matters most.

Key Question: *What makes me feel most alive—and why have I been ignoring it?*

3. The Reimagination Phase (from wondering to visioning)
Maybe I could...

Emotional Signals: Spark. Excitement. Uncertainty.
Behavioral Signs: Sketching ideas. Talking to mentors. Resurfacing dreams. Beginning something new.

This is the return of possibility. You start to dream again with your eyes wide open. You begin to imagine a new role, a new rhythm, and a new version of yourself. Ideas you had long buried begin rising again.

This is the perfect time to ask yourself three powerful questions: What would I try if I didn't fear embarrassment or failure? What if my age is not a limitation but an asset? What vision keeps returning, no matter how many times I push it aside?

Creativity and goal-setting studies show that visualizing future identity increases the likelihood of action. In other words, people act when they begin to see themselves differently. Don't dismiss your

"I may never take on an intense feat like that Cuba swim again—the training, the failures, the final victory. But I go to sleep each night with one thought: there was nothing more I could have brought to that day. That was the lesson of the Cuba Swim."
—Diana Nyad, on her fifth attempt at age 64

ideas because they feel too big. Remember that they are seeds and that you are not too old to plant them.

Key Questions: *What do I want to create, give, or experience in this next chapter—and who am I becoming in the process?*

4. The Realignment Phase (from clutter to clarity)
It's time to let go of what no longer fits.

Emotional Signals: Resolve. Clarity. Sometimes grief.
Behavioral Signs: Saying no. Restructuring life. Reallocating time and energy. Setting new boundaries.

This is the hard, beautiful work of creating margin for what matters. You start pruning—canceling what no longer aligns to make space in your calendar, and in your home.

Every time you let go of something that no longer serves you, you create space for what's finally ready to grow. By saying "not anymore," you can finally say yes to what's next.

Question: *What do I need to let go of to move forward?*

5. The Re-engagement Phase (from searching to fulfillment)
This is it. This is what I was made to do.

Emotional Signals: Peace. Joy. Flow. Meaning.
Behavioral Signs: Starting the project. Mentoring. Volunteering. Launching. Creating. Leading. Teaching. Serving.

This is the moment when your soul says yes. You have let go of unnecessary things, defined your purpose, and considered the possibility that the latter part of life could be especially fulfilling. And now you begin, not with perfection, but with presence.

This is not about going back to work. This is about going forward into impact. You become a force again, not because you're pushing, but because purpose is pulling you.

Key Question: *What am I doing now that makes time disappear and meaning return?*

The Unretirement Awakening—My Personal Experience

Unretirement is not about going back. It's about stepping forward. It's not about what you did, but what you still can do. For some, it starts with boredom. For others, it's a simple, subtle ache with days that are filled with freedom but lacking spark.

Like many, my unretirement journey began with an inner knowing: *There's still more in me.*

After selling my trade show business, the family and I moved to the Oklahoma City area, where my wife had family roots. I finally had the freedom that I expected from retirement—time to relax, breathe, and enjoy a slower pace. It felt like a well-earned pause after years of building, traveling, and pushing. I rested. I reflected. I took a breath. But before long, I knew that something was off. There was a restlessness I couldn't explain. The pace of my life had slowed, but so had the purpose.

I began paying close attention to the discomfort. I dug in—reading, journaling, and researching what others experience in this "second half." What I found was both eye-opening and deeply personal: I wasn't alone. Many were asking the same question rising in me: *What now?*

That curiosity led me to new conversations with people from numerous organizations who serve the 50+ generation. One connection led to another, and before long, small forums turned into a new vision: a live event to inspire and connect people like me. That vision became the annual *Second Half Expo*—now the largest expo in the region for individuals aged 50 and above.

There's a quote from Steve Jobs that I've come to love:

"You can't connect the dots looking forward; you can only connect them looking backward. So, you have to trust that the dots will somehow connect in your future."

That's precisely what happened for me. I didn't plan to partner with others and start another business. I simply followed the pull toward what felt right. And what unfolded was bigger, better, and more aligned than I ever could have mapped out on my own.

Also, I didn't plan to create this roadmap. I was living it. Yet every phase—*Discomfort, Reflection, Reimagination, Realignment, Re-engagement*—showed up in my own life, not as a tidy checklist but as a living journey. What began with quiet restlessness became the launch of a movement I never saw coming. Maybe it's happening for you, too.

Where Are You on the Roadmap?

- "I'm tired, restless, or drifting." → You're in **Discomfort**
- "I'm asking deeper questions and craving space." → You're in **Reflection**
- "I feel sparks of new ideas and dreams returning." → You're in **Reimagination**
- "I'm ready to simplify and create margin." → You're in **Realignment**
- "I've begun something that feels right and real." → You're in **Re-engagement**

Wherever you are, you're not stuck. You are awakening and now have the map to guide you. You no longer need to settle, wander, or wait for permission. Only one thing is left, and that is what only you can provide: movement.

Diana Nyad didn't jump back into the ocean to reclaim old glory. She swam because something deep inside her knew there was still a chapter left to write. At 64, she didn't just complete a swim—she shattered a belief, proving that life isn't over when the world says you're done. It's over when the fire inside goes out.

If you feel that fire—even as the faintest flicker—don't ignore it. That spark is the signal that you're about to begin one of the richest, most rewarding chapters of your life. Pick up the pen. Chart the course. Step back into the arena of purpose. Because you are not finished yet. This is your encore—and that encore will probably be the most meaningful thing you ever do.

The Never Retire Roadmap™

Five Phases to Realign, Reimagine, and Re-engage Your Second Half

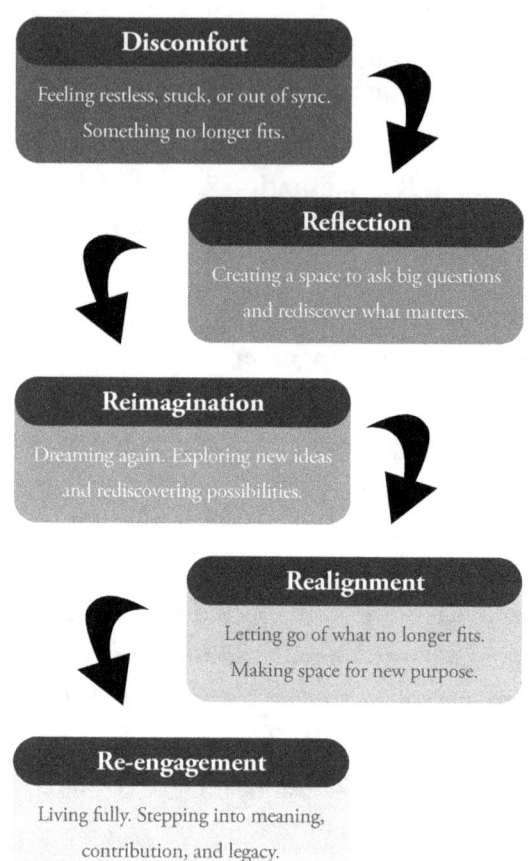

Discomfort

Feeling restless, stuck, or out of sync. Something no longer fits.

Reflection

Creating a space to ask big questions and rediscover what matters.

Reimagination

Dreaming again. Exploring new ideas and rediscovering possibilities.

Realignment

Letting go of what no longer fits. Making space for new purpose.

Re-engagement

Living fully. Stepping into meaning, contribution, and legacy.

CHAPTER 7

THE PASSION &
PURPOSE FINDER

Discover What You're Meant to Do Now—with
What You Already Have

There comes a point in life, often quietly, often unexpectedly, when the roles you've played no longer feel like home. You've done the work. Maybe you've raised the kids, built the career, played the part. You may have even succeeded more than you expected to.

But somewhere between the obligations and accomplishments, something inside you started stirring. Not loudly at first and not even in a way you could name. Just a low hum of restlessness… or maybe longing. This is not a crisis. It's an invitation.

George Lombardi: The Phone Call That Changed Everything

Dr. George Lombardi was not looking for a new mission. He was already at the pinnacle of his profession—an infectious disease specialist in New York City, treating high-profile patients and advising top hospitals. His work was respected, even elite. But sometimes purpose doesn't wait for an invitation. It arrives as a phone call.

On a Saturday night in 1989, George was settling into his new apartment when the phone rang. On the other end was a Canadian producer connected to the Missionaries of Charity. Her words were urgent: "Mother Teresa is dying. She's in Calcutta. High fever. Vomiting blood. The doctors can't find the infection. They need your help."

George offered to consult over the phone. But that wasn't enough. "They need you to come. Tomorrow." There was one problem—his passport had expired. "No matter," she said. "Be ready at 7 a.m."

The next morning, he was picked up in a wood-paneled station wagon and taken to Rockefeller Center. A State Department official opened the passport office early, issued a new passport, and had him en route to the Indian consulate. The entire staff had come in on a Sunday in full dress uniform to issue his visa. The Consul General handed it to him and spoke these sobering words: "We bestow our blessings on you. The eyes of the world are upon you."

Hours later, George boarded the Concorde, the fastest jet in the world, flying standby thanks to a businessman who gave up his seat at the urging of others.

When he arrived in Calcutta, he was taken straight to the hospital, where he concluded that the infection was related to a pacemaker recently implanted. In a makeshift operating room, with no margin for error and no previous experience, he removed the pacemaker along with the infected wire that had caused the issue. Her fever broke, and within days, she was eating again. Mother Teresa would live for another eight years.

That experience changed George. He returned to the U.S., but his heart was still in Calcutta. In the years that followed, he quietly began traveling back. He served rural clinics, mentored young doctors, and offered his expertise to the sisters who had so little but gave so much. He helped them create sterile techniques, troubleshoot infections, and provide better care for the poorest of the poor.

Finding Your Purpose

Like Dr. Lombardi, this new chapter in your life could be your most meaningful one yet. To live well, you must discover your current purpose. And then be willing, not to start over, but to start again—from a deeper and truer place.

That question—*What am I meant to do now?*—isn't a one-size-fits-all puzzle. While it's deeply personal, it's also beautifully accessible.

We tend to believe that purpose is something grand and elusive, something only the lucky or extraordinary find—some dramatic calling announced with trumpets and spotlights. But that's not how it works. Purpose is rarely loud. Rather than chase you down, it waits quietly in the background of your life until you're finally still enough to notice.

It often shows up in the patterns you thought were just coincidences and in the compliments you shrugged off. In the moment you offered comfort, and someone looked at you and said, "You have no idea how much I needed that." That was the purpose. You just didn't know it yet.

As people reach the second half of life, they often say the same thing in different ways. They may say, "I feel like there's more, but I don't know what it is." Or "I'm ready to do something that matters." Or "I want to feel alive again." And underneath those words is one deep, aching question: *Is there something in me that still has value? Is there something that I am supposed to do now?*

The answer is yes. But it won't come from looking outward. It begins by looking inward, at your own life, and listening to what it's been trying to tell you all along.

Your Story Holds the Clues

Purpose doesn't arrive like a package at your door. It emerges from your story, and if you take time to trace the threads of that story, you'll find that your life has already left you clues. They show up in the things you loved doing before someone told you to be practical. In the moments where time disappeared and you felt completely yourself. In the quiet joy of helping someone, not because you had to, but because something in you wanted to.

Your life is not a string of disconnected events. It's a narrative. And like every great story, it includes themes, characters, turning points, and meaning. When you pay attention to what your own life has been telling you—

across the years, across the pain and passion—you begin to discover the pattern. The call. The next assignment.

The five reflections below form a personal inventory—a lens to help you discern where you've been, where you are, and what may be calling you next. These are not random. These are whispers. Pause at each one and sit with the questions because this is where clarity is born.

1. PAST: *What past experiences have shaped who I am today?*

Your past is more than a memory. It's a mentor. Every trial you've survived, every success you've tasted, every failure that left a scar—they've all helped form the person you've become. The issue is no longer whether the past holds significance; rather, the focus is on understanding the message it conveys.

Begin by asking: What have I always loved doing? Think back—before careers, before expectations, before life became about responsibilities and deadlines. What did you love simply for the joy of it? Did you organize things? Write in a notebook under your blanket at night? Encourage your friends? Care for animals? Make people laugh? There's something there. That version of you wasn't pretending. You were practicing.

The passions that stirred in your childhood—before fear, failure, or the need for approval stepped in—often contain the raw ingredients of your purpose. They don't always show up in the same form today. But the energy behind them? That's still alive in you.

Now look back with purpose. Where did you grow the most? What did you have to overcome that others might still be facing? What made you weep, or roar, with conviction? Maybe you've walked through cancer, caregiving, job loss, relationship challenges, business success or even failure. These weren't detours. They were training grounds.

2. PRESENT: *What energizes me or drains me right now?*

This is where your soul begins to lean forward. What topics pull you in without effort? What makes your heart ache with compassion, or leap with joy? What do you look forward to doing, even when there's no immediate reward? What have you recently read or heard that made you think: *That! I want to be part of that.*

What gives you energy lately? What activities make time fly? When do you feel the most alive—the most "you"? It could be writing, mentoring, planning, serving, creating, organizing, or encouraging.

Likewise, take note of what exhausts you. Sometimes that exhaustion is not physical; it's emotional misalignment. So, take time to gauge your energy level and remember that it's not random. It's revealing.

You don't need to find the perfect path; you just need to notice the spark. So many people are looking for clarity when what they really need is curiosity. Let yourself be curious again.

3. PEOPLE: *Who brings out the best in me? Who might I be called to serve or help?*

Purpose isn't just about passion. It's about people. You weren't designed to walk this journey alone. The people around you hold clues, both to your strengths and your assignment.

What have you lived through that you can now offer forward? That pain you endured. That wisdom you earned. That scar you carry. That could be the very thing someone else is praying for right now, and it becomes your mission field.

Who do you feel drawn to support? Maybe it's the young people starting out, confused and hungry for guidance. Maybe it's the exhausted and overlooked caregivers. Maybe it's the underprivileged who never had a voice, or a young person who never had a father or mother figure in their life. It could be those walking through something that you survived years ago.

Whatever your lane, the point is that you're not too late. You're right on time. This life that you've lived so far on this planet was never wasted. The hard parts, the joyful parts, and even the confusing middle were preparing you to give something only you can give.

And if you still feel unsure, that's okay. Uncertainty isn't a dead end but just part of the road. People seldom start with their passion. They begin, and their passion finds them. So, take the pressure off. You don't need a vision statement; you simply need to move in small, honest ways.

4. PATTERNS: *What themes, stories, or insights keep resurfacing in my life?*

As you look closely at your story, you may see certain threads repeating—themes that won't leave you alone, questions that keep returning, insights you keep learning again and again.

Maybe you've always been the encourager or perhaps leadership keeps finding you. Maybe justice, beauty, truth, or healing keeps showing up at your doorstep. Don't dismiss these patterns as simply nuisances. They could be nudges—breadcrumbs pointing toward something you're meant to name, nurture, or give voice to.

Once you identify such patterns, you stop wandering and start awakening.

5. PURPOSE: *What might my life be preparing me to give or build next?*

This final question calls you forward. What's the assignment your life has been preparing you for?

This is where all the dots begin to connect. The experiences you've had, the passions you carry, the people who inspire you—they all converge to prepare you for what's next.

Purpose doesn't always shout. Often, it whispers, requiring that you listen closely. And it isn't always about what you enjoy. It's about what you're uniquely positioned to offer. Remember that everything you've lived through is the curriculum for your calling.

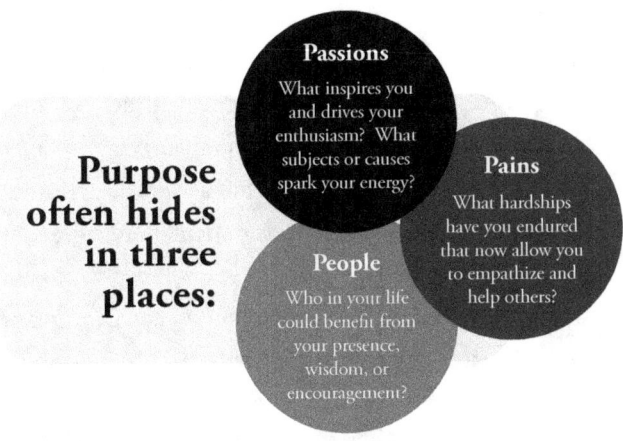

Purpose often hides in three places:

1. **Passions**: What inspires you and drives your enthusiasm? What subjects or causes spark your energy?
2. **Pains**: What hardships have you endured that now allow you to empathize and help others?
3. **People:** Who in your life could benefit from your presence, wisdom, or encouragement?

As you explore these five windows—your past, your present, your people, your patterns, and your purpose—you'll realize that you're not done yet. You're still needed here to contribute, to create, and to give something that only you can give. Your purpose hasn't retired. And neither should you.

But let's be honest: when you're standing at the crossroads of what's next, even the best framework can feel theoretical. What makes it come alive is seeing it in action. And we just saw it exemplified in the life of George Lombardi, as his purpose moved him from achievement to *impact.* From prestige to *presence.* From career to *calling.*

While you don't have to be famous like Dr. Lombardi, you do have to listen to the ache while paying attention to what's tugging at your heart. You do have to notice the moments when you say, *"Someone should do something about that..."*—and realize that maybe that someone is you.

Reflection Area	Guided Prompts
PAST: What have I always loved doing?	Think back to childhood or early adulthood—what activities made you feel alive, creative, or peaceful?
PRESENT: What energizes me now?	What topics or tasks make you lose track of time? What fills you with quiet excitement or meaning today?
PEOPLE: Who could I help, encourage, or serve?	Whose struggle do you understand deeply because of your story? Who do you feel compassion for?
PATTERNS: What themes, stories, or insights keep resurfacing in my life?	What do people regularly thank you for? What causes, roles, or moments have defined your life so far?
PURPOSE: What might my life be preparing me to give or build next?	If you could serve one cause, lead one effort, or write one final chapter—what would it be about, and why?

CHAPTER 8

THE NEVER RETIRE EQUATION™

"The meaning of life is to find your gift.
The purpose of life is to give it away."
—Pablo Picasso

We are living in one of the most remarkable periods in human history. For the first time ever, living into our eighties, nineties, and even past 100 is not the rare exception—it is becoming a common reality. Medical advances, improved nutrition, safer environments, and increased awareness of wellness have significantly extended the human lifespan over the last century.

But here's the critical question: What's the point of living longer if we're not living better? Longevity without vitality is survival. Longevity with vitality is where the adventure truly begins.

In a small village in Okinawa, Japan, elders rise each day not with a groan, but with a smile. They move deliberately, tending to their gardens, preparing food, and checking in on their neighbors. Ask them why they're still going strong at 97, 102, or even 110, and you'll likely hear one word:

Ikigai —pronounced *ee-key-guy*. Ikigai is a Japanese term that loosely translates to "reason for being." It's the thing that gets you out of bed in the morning, the inner spark that makes life worth living. It's not just about big goals or world-changing missions. It's about living with intentionality, knowing that your life still matters, and that someone still needs you.

The Alignment Audit: A Courageous Inventory

Answer these honestly:

1. **Does how I spend my time reflect what I say I value?**
   If I tracked my days for a week, would they reflect purpose or pressure?
2. **Do the people closest to me bring out my best?**
   Or am I staying in relationships out of fear, habit, or guilt?
3. **What in my life feels like friction? What feels like flow?**
   Make a list. Don't judge it—just write it.
4. **Where have I compromised too much, and forgotten who I am?**
   And what would happen if I reclaimed that part of me?
5. **If I could redesign my life from scratch today, what would stay? What would go?**
   This question alone could change everything.

Research has shown that individuals who can clearly articulate their ikigai tend to live longer and healthier lives than those who cannot. A Japanese study involving over 43,000 participants found that individuals who lacked a sense of purpose were more than twice as likely to die from cardiovascular disease than those who had a clear sense of purpose.

Blue Zones: The World's Healthiest People

In *The Blue Zones*, National Geographic explorer Dan Buettner studied five regions around the world where people consistently live the longest, healthiest lives:

- Okinawa, Japan
- Sardinia, Italy
- Ikaria, Greece
- Nicoya, Costa Rica
- Loma Linda, California

Despite being oceans and continents apart, with different diets and climates, these long-lived communities shared stunning commonalities. So what was their secret? It wasn't in a pill or a protein shake. Buettner boiled it down to a set of shared lifestyle principles—habits anyone, anywhere, can adopt.

We've distilled it down to a three-part formula:

The Never Retire Equation™
Calling + Connections + Clues = Alignment

You will remember we explored the trio of Purpose, People, and Pattern in an earlier chapter of this book. The *Never Retire Equation™* builds on that foundation, but in a more personal, discovery-based way. Here, we're not building a framework. We're listening for one.

This simple but powerful equation captures the shared DNA of the world's longest-living, most vibrant people. This formula can serve as your guide to a thriving second half of life.

1. CALLING (Ikigai): What's pulling you forward?

In Blue Zones, everyone—no matter their age—knows why they're here. In Okinawa, elders can clearly state their ikigai. One says, "I care for my great-grandchildren." Another: "I teach traditional weaving." Their answers are personal, modest, and deeply meaningful.

Ikigai isn't about achieving status or checking boxes. It's about knowing, deep down: *I still have something to give. I have a calling and a purpose.* And this isn't just about having a big mission statement or a grand plan. It's about tuning in to the tug on your heart.

You might not be able to define your calling in a sentence, but you can usually feel it. You sense it when your heart quickens around a cause, when you imagine making a difference in a specific area. When you can't shake an idea that keeps coming back.

Calling often shows up as restlessness before it becomes clarity. You don't always find it. It sometimes finds you. Pay attention to what energizes you, what breaks your heart, and what you'd do even if no one paid you. That's the voice of calling rising above the noise.

Never Retire Truth: *When you recognize your calling, your body finds a reason to stay strong.*

What's Your Ikigai?

What makes you feel alive? It might be painting, gardening, consulting, volunteering, creating, serving, encouraging, teaching, or building. It might be simple, but deeply meaningful.

2. CONNECTIONS (Moai): Who are your people?

If calling is the engine, people are the fuel. And the right people don't just support you. They unlock you. Consider the individuals who energize you, challenge you, and bring out the best in you. Who sees something in you that you sometimes forget is there?

These connections are more than social—they are directional. They help point you to where your purpose lives. Reflect on the friends, mentors, coworkers, family members, and even brief acquaintances who have said or done something that stuck with you. Often, our future is found in the echoes of these relationships.

In Blue Zone cultures, no one ages alone. In Okinawa, people form *moais*—tight-knit support groups that stick together for life. They meet, eat, laugh, grieve, and celebrate—side by side. In Sardinia, men gather daily in the village square just to laugh and talk. In Loma Linda, potlucks and faith-based communities form a relational safety net that sustains people into their 90s and beyond.

Science confirms what many cultures have practiced intuitively:

- Strong social ties lower the risk of chronic disease, support faster physical recovery, and boost immune function.
- They protect against depression and cognitive decline, helping older adults stay mentally agile and emotionally resilient.
- Even survival after surgery, loss, or health crises improves when community and family are involved.

In contrast, social isolation is dangerous. A major meta-analysis involving over 300,000 participants found that isolation increases the risk of early death by about 29%, while loneliness and living alone also significantly elevated mortality risk.

These findings aren't just statistics. They are a compelling case: the essence of flourishing in the second half of life isn't found in silence. It's found in connection. And a life lived in community is measurably healthier.

Never Retire Truth: *You were never meant to do this alone. You're designed to flourish in community, purpose, and shared vitality.*

Who's in Your Moai?

Who knows your story and walks beside you? If you feel disconnected, this is your moment to rebuild. Life's not meant to be solo. Start with two or three people you can text, talk to, or pray with each week. Then nurture those roots.

3. CLUES (Daily Flow): What patterns keep resurfacing?

Your life has been quietly leaving a trail of clues. Patterns. Recurring threads woven through your days. These are not accidents—they are indicators. So, pay close attention to what keeps resurfacing.

- What do you keep getting pulled toward?
- What do people come to you for help with?
- What do you naturally notice or get excited about?
- When do you lose track of time?

These recurring threads are not random. They're clues to your flow and the tapestry of your calling. Follow them with curiosity and courage.

Clues lead to patterns. Patterns create flow, and flow fuels lasting energy.

Never Retire Truth: *Longevity is not about extreme bursts of effort, but about consistency over time.*

Your life becomes aligned when you bring together your *Calling*—what matters most to you, your *Connections*—the people who energize and support you, and your *Clues*—the patterns and hints life keeps showing you. And when you are aligned, your second half will become your strongest, most purpose-filled season yet.

What's Your Daily Flow?

Are you moving naturally? Resting deeply? Engaging meaningfully? Do your days drain you or restore you? What rhythms are missing that could bring strength, joy, or calm?

Designing Your Own Blue Zone

You don't need to relocate to a Greek island. You can build your version of a Blue Zone, right where you are. It starts with asking three life-changing questions:

1. **What's my calling now?** (that which stirs my soul)
2. **Who are my people?** (the people who fuel and shape me)
3. **What are the clues?** (the recurring patterns and gifts that whisper direction)

Alignment occurs when your values, actions, environment, vision, and calendar are not in conflict, but in harmony. It is living your life without having to change between your identity, beliefs, and activities.

✥ Activation Spotlight

Flourishing Is Not a Luxury. It's Your Second Half Advantage

What Breakthrough Research Reveals About Where Your Best Years Really Begin

What does it mean to flourish in life, especially in the Second Half? For years, we've been told that success looks like a fat retirement account, a golf course membership, and long days with nothing urgent to do. However, a groundbreaking international study recently overturned that idea.

In the most extensive global study of its kind, researchers from Gallup, Harvard, Baylor, and the Center for Open Science asked a daring question: *What if we could measure how well people are living, and not just how long?*

This led to the Global Flourishing Study, a $43.4 million, five-year project tracking over 200,000 individuals across 22 countries. Unlike most research that focuses on disease or income alone, this study measured six dimensions of whole-person well-being.

1. Happiness and Life Satisfaction
2. Mental and Physical Health
3. Meaning and Purpose
4. Character and Virtue
5. Close Social Relationships
6. Financial and Material Stability

One of the most striking trends? In many countries, including the United States, older adults in their 60s and 70s reported higher flourishing scores than younger generations. While younger adults (especially those aged 18–29) struggled most with life satisfaction, purpose, and mental health, older adults expressed stronger relationships, steadier outlooks, and deeper meaning.

The takeaway? Flourishing doesn't fade with age. It often grows. This directly reinforces the *Never Retire* movement's core belief: that the second half of life isn't about stepping aside. It's about stepping fully into purpose. So ask yourself:

- Am I living with purpose?
- Do I have a reason to get out of bed in the morning?
- Am I engaging in meaningful connection and contribution?
- Am I nurturing habits that ground me, challenge me, and lift me?

PART III
POWER

You still have more in the tank—more strength, more story, more influence.

CHAPTER 9

THE UNSTOPPABLE MINDSET FOR LIFE'S SECOND HALF

"I am always doing that which I cannot do,
in order that I may learn how to do it."
—Pablo Picasso

The Farmer Who Redefined What's Possible

In 1983, Australia hosted its first-ever ultramarathon: a grueling 543.7-mile race stretching from Sydney to Melbourne. The starting line buzzed with anticipation as elite athletes gathered—young, lean, highly trained, and equipped with the best running gear money could buy.

And then Cliff Young stepped to the starting line. He was 61 years old. A potato farmer, wearing overalls, work boots, and no dentures—he later said they rattled when he ran. Most people thought he was joking, but Cliff wasn't there to joke. He was there to run.

From the beginning, Cliff ran at a slow and loping pace—what would later be called the "Young Shuffle." By the end of the first day, he was far behind the rest of the field. The other runners followed a proven strategy: run hard all day, then sleep for six hours.

Cliff mistakenly woke up at 2 am. Not knowing any better, he started running again, taking the lead while all the others slept. Realizing he was now in the lead, he made a decision to forgo sleep as a strategy. After a little over 5½ days, with no more sleep, he crossed the finish line in first place, 10 hours faster than the runner who came in second.

Before the race, he told reporters that he had spent years chasing sheep on foot across vast stretches of land, sometimes for days at a time. During the race, he said he imagined he was running after sheep, trying to outrun an incoming storm.

Cliff Young didn't just break records. He broke assumptions.
He didn't have younger legs or modern gear. What he had was a different mindset. He didn't know the standard rules, so he didn't limit himself by them.

Cliff's story reminds us that your mindset isn't a background feature of your life—it's the operating system. It determines what you believe is possible, what you're willing to try, how you deal with setbacks, and whether you finish the race at all.

Mindset Is the Multiplier

If there's one thing that will determine the quality of your second half, it's not your finances, your location, or even your health. It's your mindset. It doesn't just influence what you do. It amplifies the meaning, energy, and direction behind it. Change your mindset, and everything else begins to change with it.

That's the power of a mindset shift. It's like flipping a light switch in a dark room. Suddenly, you can see clearly, and you recognize new paths. What once felt like a limitation now feels like an invitation.

> You don't need to change everything in your life. You just need to change how you think about everything in your life.

The Never Retire Mindset

The remaining chapters in this book will have one thing in common: they only work if you approach them with the right mindset. If you shift your thinking, you open new doors. If you don't, even the best strategies will feel out of reach.

Mindset is how you frame challenges. It's how you see time, how you define success, and how you move through setbacks. It's the lens through which everything else is filtered.

Fixed Mindset vs. Growth Mindset

One of the most well-known insights into mindset comes from the work of Dr. Carol Dweck, who introduced the concepts of a *fixed mindset* versus a *growth mindset*. Her research found that how we see ourselves—whether we believe our potential is fixed or evolving—determines how we grow, change, and persevere.

People with a fixed mindset believe their abilities and intelligence are static. They avoid challenges, fear failure, and often plateau early. But those with a growth mindset believe they can improve through effort, learning, and resilience. They embrace challenges, persist through obstacles, and see failure as a springboard, not a stop sign.

In one striking example from her research, children given challenging puzzles responded in very different ways. Some gave up quickly, saying things like, "I'm not good at this." Others leaned in with curiosity: "I love a challenge. I want to try again." What made the difference? Not intelligence. Not skill. Mindset!

And it doesn't stop in childhood. A groundbreaking 23-year Yale study found that older adults with a positive mindset about aging lived, on average, 7.5 years longer than those with negative beliefs. The longevity benefit of such positivity exceeded that of maintaining normal blood pressure, healthy weight, quitting smoking, or regular exercise.

Why? Because mindset drives action, and action shapes outcomes. We don't respond to life as it is—we respond to life as we perceive it. The stories we tell ourselves, the scripts we follow, and the beliefs we repeat silently each day become the lens through which we interpret opportunities, challenges, and even our own worth.

Opportunity Mindset

One of the most important mindset shifts to embrace in the second half of life is this: opportunity doesn't always knock. Sometimes it whispers.

That truth found me late one evening. I wasn't reading a leadership manual or some transformational biography—just casually flipping through a book before bed, not expecting much. But suddenly one line seemed to leap off the page and shout: *"Opportunities rarely come at opportune times!"*

Feeling an internal jolt, I sat up straight. It was exactly what I needed in the moment. That single sentence reframed how I think, and how I listen. It reminded me that mindset isn't just about positivity or grit. It's about attunement. It's the inner alignment that lets you hear the quiet knock when opportunity passes by... and gives you the courage to open the door.

Here's the reality: the most life-changing opportunities don't arrive when everything is calm, clear, and convenient. They often show up when you're juggling too many things, fighting distractions, or putting out fires. They come

What flag of opportunity have you noticed during the past week or two?

Does it align with your priorities? If so, write down the next few steps for taking advantage of it.

disguised—as interruptions, detours, or even problems. But in the distance, if you look closely, you'll often see it: a little flag of opportunity waving, inviting you to take notice.

That's exactly what happened to me with this book. The idea for *Never Retire* wasn't born out of leisure or planning. It came amid a busy life. I had other projects, other responsibilities, and more than a few reasons to ignore it. But that sentence lit a spark. I paused, evaluated, and then asked: "Am I approaching this with the right mindset and does it align with what matters most to me? Is this one of those moments I'll regret missing if I let it pass?" As soon as I said yes, I rearranged my schedule and made space. I followed the flag. That's how this book was born.

When opportunity waves at you, don't assume it will come back later. Stop. Look. Evaluate your mindset. If it aligns with your purpose, make room for it, even if your timing feels off. Because opportunities rarely come at opportune times. But when they do come, they just might change your life.

Tying It All Together

Cliff Young didn't win that ultramarathon with strategy or speed. He won because he thought differently. He didn't accept the limits everyone else believed were non-negotiable. And once he broke the record, others followed. That's the power of mindset—not just to change your own life, but to create ripple effects.

The rest of this book is filled with strategies, stories, and tools. Yet none of them will matter if your mindset is stuck. Flip the script and challenge the assumptions. Your second half isn't governed by your age. It's governed by your attitude. And your mindset—that's the place where everything begins.

Reflection:
What false finish lines have you accepted because of someone else's mindset?

What would happen if you started believing again? Dreaming again? Trying again?

The word "retire" originates from the French *retirer* and means to withdraw, pull back, or retreat. Is that what your life was meant to be? A slow fade into the background? A quiet retreat from purpose? No! You were born for more.

Embrace the Never Retire Mindset

- Your best years are ahead, not behind you.
- Retirement isn't an age—it's a mindset.
- You don't retire FROM something—you retire TO something.
- True fulfillment comes from staying engaged.

CHAPTER 10

THE POWER OF WORDS

If we want to change the way we live,
we must first change the way we speak.

Your Words Carry Power

What if the single most overlooked factor in how we experience the second half of life wasn't your health, your money, or even your circumstances, but your words? Yes, your words. What you say to others. What you say about yourself. What you say when you think no one is listening. Because here's the truth: someone is always listening. You are!

You might not realize it, but every day you're narrating your life out loud and in your head. That narration is doing more than just filling space. It's shaping how you think, feel, and live. The words you use carry enormous power. They can energize you or exhaust you. Build you up or break you down. Push you forward or hold you back.

In this chapter, we'll expose the silent influence of outdated vocabulary, transform tired phrases into empowering language, and shine a light on the most important conversation you'll ever have: the one you have with yourself.

The Science of Words

Scientific evidence shows that the way you describe your life directly shapes how you experience it. We noticed earlier that research from Yale University found that people with positive perceptions of aging live an average of 7.5 years longer than those with negative views. Your words about aging, even your jokes, aren't harmless. They're powerful predictors of how you live and how long you live. Your vocabulary is not just descriptive. It's prescriptive.

When you speak of life as exciting, full of possibilities, and rich with meaning, you tell your brain to look for opportunities. If you talk in terms of decline and limitation, you train your brain to shrink your world. Words create energy, energy creates action, and action creates momentum.

The Newly Revised Dictionary for Aging Well

Culturally, we've inherited a vocabulary of decline, limitation, and even irrelevance. We hear outdated words and phrases like: *Old. Over the hill. Senior moment. Past your prime.*

The Power of Words

Language matters. If you talk about aging like it's a disease, you'll experience it as decline. If you speak of it as a mission, a gift, a calling, you'll live accordingly.

Here are some of the most common outdated terms we hear, and how to flip them into something life-giving:

Old Word/ Phrase	Empowering Alternative
Old	Older, Seasoned, Experienced, Wise
Elderly	Wise Generation, Prime Timers, Legends
Retired	Rewired, Repurposed, Thriving in the 2nd Half
Senior Citizen	Modern Elder, Trailblazer, Mentor-in-Chief
Over the Hill	On Top of the Mountain, Peak Performer
Past Your Prime	Hitting Your Stride, Entering Your Legacy Years
Empty Nester	Freedom Explorer, New Chapter Adventurer
Midlife Crisis	Midlife Awakening, Purpose Shift
Senior Moment	Wisdom Pause, Reflection Break
Growing Old	Growing Bold, Growing Wise

Never Retire

Also, transform these outdated expressions:

Retire This Phrase	Replace With This One
You can't teach an old dog new tricks.	*You don't become an old dog until you refuse to learn new tricks.*
I'm having a senior moment.	*I'm pausing for clarity.*
Act your age.	*Act the age you feel inside.*
Slowing down with age.	*Gearing up for what's next.*
It's too late to start now.	*Now is the perfect time to begin.*
I'm over the hill.	*I'm standing on the peak with the best view.*

Take a moment to reflect: Which of these phrases do you catch yourself using? Which ones do you hear from others? And which new word or phrase might you try on today? The way you talk about your life shapes your reality.

The Power of Everyday Responses

Let's start with one of the most common questions we ask each other: "How are you doing?" You've probably heard it hundreds of times in your life. Most people answer automatically and without much thought: *Fine. Okay. Still kicking. Vertical for now.*

These answers don't just lack enthusiasm. They reflect a mindset of survival, not vitality. But something powerful happens when we pause and lean in.

I started doing a little experiment. When someone says, "I'm fine," I pause and ask, "How are you *really* doing, [insert name]?" This approach often leads the person to provide a more genuine response as they become more open.

In a world where everyone is moving fast and wearing masks, that one word—*really*—has the power to invite honesty, connection, and even healing. Try it. Say it with compassion, not interrogation. *How are you really doing?* You'll be surprised what people are carrying just beneath the surface, waiting for someone to notice.

Now flip the mirror. When someone asks you how you're doing, don't default to tired scripts. Speak a future truth—one that pulls you forward. Try something like: *Grateful and growing. Fantastic—my life is full. Blessed. Getting better every day.*

You'll feel the shift in your spirit. And others will feel it too.

Self-Talk: The Conversation That Changes Everything

Now, let's go deeper. There is one voice that individuals hear more than any other: their own. This voice is not limited to spoken words; it includes the internal dialogues within one's mind. This internal voice serves as the narrator of an individual's thoughts and inner world.

Research indicates we think tens of thousands of thoughts daily, often negatively. Self-criticism, doubt, and defeat are common. This inner voice whispers constantly, criticizing us for mistakes: *I'm such an idiot. Why bother? I'll mess it up.*

Dr. Shad Helmstetter, in *What to Say When You Talk to Yourself*, powerfully explores how our self-talk shapes our lives, and how many of our internal messages stem from negative and habitual programming. Media sources often cite mindset researchers who suggest that we might experience tens of thousands of thoughts daily, many of which are negative. While the figures vary, common estimates place daily negative thoughts at around 60–80%, reminding us of the critical importance of intentionally rewiring how we speak to ourselves.

Your inner dialogue can either uplift or undermine you. Negative self-talk includes thoughts like, *I'm too old to change. I never finish anything. What's the point now? I've messed up again.*

Fortunately, you can reprogram this voice. New, positive thoughts might include, *I can learn. My best years are ahead. I have wisdom from experience. I'm just getting started. All games are won in the second half.*

Start catching the words you say to yourself. Challenge and replace them now because eventually your self-talk becomes your self-belief.

And if you want a playful way to help someone else interrupt their inner critic? Try this line the next time you hear someone continually criticizing themselves: *"Hey, would you quit being so hard on my friend?"* You'll be surprised how many people smile, pause, and say, "Thank you... I needed that."

The Habit of Complaining & Fussing

There is a story about a man who decided to become a monk. He joined a remote monastery and adhered to a strict vow of silence for three years, with the condition that he could only speak two words at the end of each year. After completing the first year, he told the head monk, "Hard bed." At the end of the second year, he said, "Bad food." By the end of the third year, he stated, "I quit." The head monk didn't miss a beat. He simply shrugged and replied, "Well, that's just fine. All you've done is complain since the day you arrived!"

Funny story—but it also hits a little close to home. Because even in silence, some of us still carry a habit of complaining or fussing. It's woven into our thoughts, our relationships, and even our humor. And it slowly drains our joy and the joy of those around us.

We've all been there. A few complaints here and a little venting there. However, when it becomes a lifestyle, it begins to steal your energy and joy. Complaining focuses your attention on problems. Gratitude shifts your focus to possibility.

The 24-Hour No Complaining Challenge

Try going a whole day without a single complaint. If you catch yourself starting to say something negative, reframe it. Instead of "I hate this cold weather," say "This crisp air wakes me up." Instead of "I'm tired of getting older," say "I love the wisdom I've gained." The more you practice, the more natural it becomes.

Another habit that needs to be retired is fussing, especially between spouses, close friends, or coworkers. It's not yelling; it's subtle and almost invisible actions like sighing before correcting someone, jabbing at a friend's lateness, or habitually pointing out mistakes.

> Some people will argue at the drop of a hat...and then argue over who gets to drop the hat!

Fussing is low-grade negativity that creates emotional strain over time. It leads to walking on eggshells and dodging each other's minor criticisms. Most people don't even realize they do it, as it becomes their default behavior.

How to Eliminate the Habit of Complaining & Fussing:

- **Catch yourself.** Start noticing when you pick at small things.
- **Ask: Is this helpful?** Will this improve our relationship or just satisfy my need to be right?

- **Replace with kindness.** Build the habit of offering grace instead of correction.

The Power of What You Don't Say

So far, we've talked a lot about what to say. But there's another kind of power—one that comes from restraint. From choosing *not* to speak certain words aloud.

I've noticed something in my own life: when I'm overwhelmed—whether by a big project, too many obligations, or a season of emotional pressure—I often start vocalizing that weight. I'll say things like, "This is so much," or "I'm buried," or "I'm drained."

I've noticed that talking about difficulties makes them feel heavier. However, if I stay silent and shift my focus or just breathe through it, the weight lessens, and my energy returns.

There's real science behind this. Verbalizing negative emotions, especially repeatedly, can actually reinforce and amplify their impact on your nervous system. In contrast, choosing not to give those thoughts airtime can help regulate your emotional state and give your body space to reset.

Research shows that what we dwell on, we strengthen. So while honest expression has its place, habitual complaining or rehearsing negative emotions can wire your brain for stress. Silence, reframing, or redirection isn't denial—it's discipline. It's giving your nervous system a chance to calm, recover, and move forward.

Another example: I've caught myself saying out loud, "Whew, I'm tired." Sometimes multiple times a day. But here's the twist—I've started talking back. I'll immediately respond with, "No I'm not. I feel great!" And guess what? I usually do feel better, and my body automatically responds to the new command. My energy shifts, and even my posture improves.

Words are seeds. And sometimes, silence is the best way to keep weeds from growing.

Your Words Create Your World

Your words impact your thoughts and actions. Reflect on whether they promote positivity or negativity. Be mindful, as your words shape your choices and path. Focus on constructive communication for growth and future potential.

The Power of Words

Old Phrase	New Empowering Phrase
Retirement	Reinvention
Old Age	Prime Age
Senior Moment	Growth Moment / Pause to Reflect
Over the Hill	Above the Clouds
Empty Nest	Open Nest (Filled with Freedom)
Set in Your Ways	Seasoned in Wisdom
Washed Up	Warming Up
Overqualified	Uniquely Qualified
Can't Teach an Old Dog New Tricks	You're Never Too Old to Learn
Golden Years (Passive)	Platinum Years (Rare and Valuable)
Act Your Age	Live Beyond Limits
Elderly	Elder / Sage / Wise Elder
Anti-Aging	Pro-Living / Age Embracing
Senior Citizen	Experienced Citizen / Vibrant Citizen
Aging Workforce	Experienced Workforce
Midlife Crisis	Midlife Catalyst / Midlife Awakening
Senior Discount	Wisdom Dividend
Slowing Down	Hitting Your Stride
Getting Old	Getting Bold
Too Late to Start	Perfect Time to Begin
Second Childhood	Second Wind / Encore Season
I'm Past My Prime	My Prime Is Just Beginning
Aging Gracefully (Passive Tone)	Aging Powerfully / Aging Purposefully
I've Done My Time	My Time Is Now
Out to Pasture	Out to Possibility
Old School	Timeless Wisdom
End of the Road	Beginning of a New Road
Used to Be	Becoming More Every Day
In Decline	On the Rise
Can't Keep Up	Setting My Own Pace

CHAPTER 11

STRUGGLE: WHY RESISTANCE MAKES YOU STRONGER

"Fishermen know that the sea is dangerous and the storm fearsome, but they have never found these dangers sufficient reason for remaining ashore. When the storm comes—when night falls—what's worse: the danger or the fear of danger? Give me reality, the danger itself."

—Vincent van Gogh

I was having a rough day in business. You know the kind. One of those days when everything feels heavier than it should. Problems stack up, obstacles loom larger, and you start to question if your efforts are yielding results.

> "Smooth seas do not make skillful sailors."
> —African proverb

On that day, I picked up the phone and called my friend Bryan. I was, to be honest, looking for a little sympathy. What I got instead was a paradigm shift.

Bryan, a seasoned entrepreneur, has built his life around starting businesses and growing things from the ground up.

As a hobby, he also grows vegetables in the greenhouse he built in his backyard.

Bryan patiently listened to me without interruption for at least twenty minutes as I unloaded my frustrations. When I finally ran out of steam, and after a long pause of silence, Bryan proceeded to share something that I have never forgotten.

He began by telling me about his microgreens, of all things. He told me how, in his greenhouse, he places a tray directly over the microgreens after planting the seeds. At first, it sounds counterintuitive. Wouldn't that block their growth? But no. The weight of the tray, Bryan explained, forces the tiny seedlings to push upward with strength. It builds resilience in their stems, making them sturdier and more vibrant when they finally break through the surface. Without that struggle, the greens would grow tall but weak, unable to stand upright.

Bryan then let out a big laugh, not unkindly but with the laughter of someone who knows life's tough truths. He said, "Bob, I've had to reinvent myself at least six times since starting this entrepreneurial journey."

He then rattled off, almost like a checklist of chaos, several things that were currently happening in his world. An employee recently stole his business concept and was now competing with him. His two top account leaders resigned on the same day and left for the Caribbean. He lost a major account worth half a million dollars annually, through no fault of his own. And to top it off, a pending lawsuit against the employee who betrayed him was eating up time and energy.

Bryan could have been bitter, but instead, he sounded alive. As I listened to him, my own troubles started to feel strangely lighter. He had learned what so many of us resist: struggle builds strength. When you understand this, everything changes.

The Greenhouse Effect: Embrace the Weight

Bryan's greenhouse metaphor is more than a gardening tip. It's a life principle. The weight over the seedlings doesn't crush them. It strengthens them.

Likewise, the pressures in your life—the unexpected setbacks, the disappointments, the betrayals, the financial strains, the physical limitations that come with aging— they are not meant to bury you. They are intended to build you.

It's the resistance that produces resilience. It's the weight that creates the warrior. This is not theory. It is seen throughout nature, business, and human experience. Athletes who never train against resistance never build strength, and people who never encounter hardship never develop depth.

Bryan went on to tell me about the article he had recently read concerning old silos in Kansas. Over the years, trees would sometimes sprout inside them. But once the walls came down, these trees were exposed to the Kansas winds for the first time, and before long, they toppled. Why? Because they had grown in a protected environment. They had never faced the winds that would have strengthened their trunks and deepened their roots. The very protection that allowed them to grow tall had also left them fragile.

What a powerful lesson for life. Ease and comfort may feel good in the moment, but they do not prepare us for life's inevitable storms. Struggle, on the other hand, deepens our roots, preparing us to stand strong when the winds come—and they will come.

Psychologists refer to this concept in clinical settings as *Stress Inoculation Training*—exposing people to manageable stress to build future resilience.

A foundational study led by Dr. Mark Seery at the University at Buffalo found that people who experienced moderate adversity in their lives reported better outcomes—like higher life satisfaction and emotional resilience—than those with without adversity. It suggests that overcoming manageable obstacles strengthens us, preparing us to thrive when life gets harder.

Reframing: Turning Pressure into Power

A powerful strategy for handling overwhelm isn't to push harder—it's to reframe. When fatigue or frustration sets in, our first instinct is often to grind through. But science shows that how we interpret a challenge matters just as much as the challenge itself. Instead of labeling the situation as *impossible* or *too much,* start by noticing your language.

Replace defeatist thoughts like *"I can't do this"* with curious or compassionate reframes like:

- *This is hard—but I've faced hard things before.*
- *What would it look like to solve just one piece of this right now?*

The brain responds differently to challenge when it's met with possibility instead of panic. Reframing doesn't deny difficulty. It reshapes how we move through it.

Struggle Prepares You for What's Next

Rather than serving as punishment, struggle acts as a vital preparation for what's ahead. In fact, behind nearly every story of reinvention lies a period of adversity met head-on with courage and action. These narratives reveal how obstacles, far from being mere setbacks, become the very crucible in which growth, resilience, and new possibilities are forged.

There are numerous cases of individuals who have changed their circumstances after facing setbacks. The following are three examples.

Colonel Harland Sanders: Fired, Rejected—Then Reinvented at Age 65

Before Colonel Sanders became the face of Kentucky Fried Chicken, he lived a long life full of failure, frustration, and false starts. He worked as a farmhand, a streetcar conductor, a railroad fireman, a lawyer (disbarred), an insurance salesman (fired), and a ferry boat operator—just to name a few. By age 65, his roadside restaurant had closed due to a new interstate bypass. With nothing but his social security check and a pressure cooker, he hit the road to pitch his fried chicken recipe to restaurants.

> Those who dare to see with their hearts often create what the world eventually sees with its eyes.

He was rejected 1,009 times before finally persuading one restaurant to take a chance. That spark led to a fire, and within a decade, he had built one of the most recognizable franchises in the world. He wasn't a youthful startup founder. He was a man in his sixties who turned rejection into a reinvention that served meals to the world.

Laura Ingalls Wilder: A Later-Life Legacy

Laura Ingalls Wilder, beloved author of the *Little House* series, didn't publish her first book until the age of 65. She began writing late in life, using a pencil and writing on both sides of yellow tablet paper to save money. Her first manuscript, a memoir titled *Pioneer Girl*, was rejected by every publisher she submitted it to.

But Wilder didn't give up. Instead, she reworked her material into fiction for younger readers—what became the *Little House* books. Despite being told that writing for children was a waste of time, she persevered. Her series went on to sell over 60 million copies and has been translated into more than 40 languages.

Today, the *Little House* legacy—including books, TV adaptations, and merchandise—has been estimated to be worth over $100 million.

Walt Disney: Fired for "Lacking Imagination"

Early in his career, Walt Disney was fired from a newspaper job because, as his editor claimed, he "lacked imagination and had no good ideas." One of his first companies, *Laugh-O-Gram Studios*, went bankrupt. He was told Mickey Mouse would terrify women. Later, studios rejected *Snow White*, believing a full-length animated film would never work. But Disney's setbacks never defined him. His vision did.

He dreamed bigger than his obstacles—envisioning not just movies, but immersive worlds where imagination could come to life. His determination to keep creating changed the world of storytelling forever. He didn't just overcome adversity. He used it as a blueprint for building the most magical company on earth.

Years after his passing, Walt's widow, Lillian Disney, was approached at the grand opening of Disney World. A guest remarked, "It's too bad Walt didn't live to see this." After a long pause, she replied softly, "Oh, but he did see it. And that's why you're seeing it."

From Wounds to Wisdom

These stories aren't fairy tales. They're real-life case studies in grit-fueled reinvention. Each of these now-famous individuals faced rejection, disappointment, and devastating setbacks. In each case, struggle sparked reinvention. Rather than being a signal to quit, the hard days are a signal to dig deeper and to push through the weight, like Bryan's microgreens. To let the winds strengthen us, like trees growing in open fields.

Bryan said it best at the end of our conversation that day: *"Life and struggle are synonymous. Whether you're an insect, an animal, or a human, struggle is part of life. Don't reject or regret the struggles—they are like war injuries that become medals of honor."*

If you're facing struggles right now, take heart. This is not the end of your story. This is the middle of your masterpiece. Push against the weight, like Bryan's microgreens. Let the winds strengthen you, like the trees outside the silo. Embrace the scars, like medals of honor.

You are not defined by the struggle. Your response to it defines you—and your response is what turns struggle into strength.

CHAPTER 12

LAUNCH A POWER PROJECT™

Because a man can't just sit around!

The Man in the Lawn Chair

On July 2, 1982, Larry Walters, a 33-year-old truck driver from Los Angeles, did something that made history—and headlines. Armed with a lawn chair, 42 helium-filled weather balloons, some sandwiches, 2 liters of Coca-Cola, a camera, a parachute, and a pellet gun, Larry launched himself into the sky. His goal was modest: float peacefully 30 feet above his backyard, enjoy the view, and then gently float back down.

Reality had other plans. As soon as the ropes holding him down broke loose, Larry shot into the air as though released from a cannon. He rapidly ascended to 16,000 feet, eventually drifting into controlled airspace near Long Beach Airport. A startled pilot radioed air traffic control: "Uh...I just passed a guy in a lawn chair...with a gun."

Larry had intended to shoot balloons, one at a time, when it was time to gently descend, but he accidentally dropped the pellet gun. Eventually, he drifted into power lines, causing a 20-minute electricity blackout in parts of Long Beach.

He was immediately arrested upon landing. When reporters asked him why he did it, Larry gave an answer that was both absurd and insightful: "Well, a man can't just sit around."

Absurd? Absolutely. Dangerous? Definitely. But here's the uncomfortable truth: Larry was right!

A man (or woman) can't just sit around. Not with balloons. Not with boredom, not with "used to" stories, and too many days that look the same. You need something better than a lawn chair and a parachute. You need a project.

Some of the happiest, most vibrant people I know live by this simple principle: *Always have a project.* When one project ends, they start another. When challenges arise, they see them as projects to solve. When life slows down, they create new projects to stay engaged. Projects become their rhythm of life.

The next great chapter of your life won't begin with clarity. It will begin with action.

A project is the bridge between purpose and action. It's about taking your vision and bringing it into reality. And here's the best part: there is no limit to what your project can be.

Power Projects™: The Antidote to Sitting Around

A Power Project™ is a purposeful pursuit that breathes momentum, creativity, and meaning into the second half of life. It's not merely a task; it's a commitment to growth, creativity, and contribution.

It's a mission—something with purpose and a pulse. It's a focused endeavor that pulls you forward with purpose, stretches your strengths, and awakens your creativity.

Without a Power Project™, you risk drifting, like Larry. You wander through life wondering why something feels off. But when you have something meaningful to work on, your brain, your body, and your spirit all benefit. Having a goal-directed activity can increase life satisfaction and mental sharpness while reducing depression and cognitive decline.

A Power Project™ gives you:

- Direction when you're drifting
- Excitement when things feel flat
- Courage when you've grown cautious
- And a deeply satisfying sense of "I'm not done yet."

Three Types of Power Projects™

Not all projects are created equal. Some are sprints. Some are journeys. And some become your life's work in the second half. Here's a framework to help you plan, pace, and pursue the right kind of project for the season you're in.

117

1. Momentum Projects *(1–7 Days)*
Quick wins that spark confidence, creativity, and joy.

Momentum projects can be completed in a few hours, a weekend, or a single week. They are powerful because they get you moving while rebuilding your confidence.

Examples:

- Write and mail a handwritten encouragement note to someone
- Invite someone over whom you've been meaning to reconnect with
- Declutter one space: a closet, drawer, or garage shelf
- Plant flowers in your front yard or start a small herb garden
- Cook a new recipe and share it with a neighbor
- Record a short video message for your future grandchildren
- Print and frame a favorite family photo
- Visit a nursing home or shut-in with a small gift
- Clean out your car and write down your next three goals while you do it
- Take a one-day "Tech Sabbath" and reflect on your priorities

Why they matter: These are small but significant. They restore the joy of finishing something. Even completing something simple, like cleaning out a garage, will deliver a surge of positive emotions. If you're stuck or stalled, a Momentum Project is your best next step.

2. Quarterly Projects *(90 Days)*
A season-long focus that gives purpose and measurable progress.

These are more meaningful efforts, substantial enough to challenge you, but not overwhelming. These create rhythm, progress, and fulfillment. We recommend aiming for one of these projects every 3 months.

Examples:

- Take a 12-week course in something new (writing, photography, technology, a language)
- Create a personal cookbook of family recipes and stories
- Plan and execute a small group study or book club
- Organize a multi-generational family gathering or weekend retreat
- Walk 100 miles over 90 days (track and celebrate it!)
- Sort, digitize, and archive your family photos and videos
- Write and gift a "Life Lessons" journal to your children or grandchildren
- Visit and volunteer weekly at a nonprofit that aligns with your heart
- Interview five older people in your community and compile their life advice

Why they matter: Quarterly projects keep you focused. They are big enough to matter and small enough to finish. They fit naturally with the seasons of life and allow you to build sustainable momentum. You'll be amazed at what you can accomplish with just 90 days of intentional effort.

3. Legacy Projects *(1 Year or More)*
Deep, purposeful pursuits that shape your impact and story.

These are your dreams that will take a year or even a few years to complete—your second-half masterpieces that require long-term vision. Legacy Projects usually touch on your deepest values. They are worth your time, energy, and perseverance. And they often bless others for years to come.

Examples:

- Write and self-publish a book or devotional
- Create a video series or podcast sharing wisdom from your life and faith
- Launch a mentoring group focused on a cause that matters to you
- Restore a meaningful old car, piece of furniture, or heirloom
- Build a personal or family "Legacy Binder" with wills, instructions, letters, and values
- Research and write your extended family's generational history and stories
- Start a nonprofit that helps people in a specific stage of life (widows, veterans, youth)

- Turn a lifelong skill into a teaching curriculum and train others
- Build a creative studio or quiet retreat space that invites reflection and legacy work

Why they matter: Legacy Projects stretch you, and they require more than enthusiasm. They demand vision, resilience, and wise planning. They take time, but they're worth it because they outlive you and become part of the story you pass on.

All three kinds of Power Projects™ matter. So, start where you are and don't stay still.

The Rubber Band Principle: Vision vs. Reality

Here's the truth that no one tells you about bold projects: the bigger the vision, the greater the tension. In *The Fifth Discipline*, Peter Senge shares the metaphor of a rubber band stretched between two hands:

- One hand holds your *vision*—where you want to be.
- The other holds your *current reality*—where you are now.
- The tension between the two? That's called *creative tension.*

This tension doesn't go away on its own. When you elevate your vision to something bigger, you're being stretched. You then have two choices: *let go of the vision* and pull it down to match reality. Or, *move reality upward* toward your vision through faith and action.

Tension is the engine of progress, but it's uncomfortable. Here's how to use it:

- **Name it.** Say, "This is creative tension. I'm stretching."
- **Normalize it.** Growth always feels awkward before it feels powerful.
- **Act through it.** Take one step forward. Then another.
- **Choose the vision.** Again. And again.

The Day I Was Told to Dial It Back

While working on this very book, I interviewed a publishing consultant. I laid out the full vision, encompassing a book, workbook, assessment, movement, and a legacy message.

After reviewing it all, he said something that surprised me: "You should dial this back. Cut it in half. Make it smaller and narrower." And I'll be honest—for a moment I wavered. The logic was sound: less complexity, less cost, and less risk.

But suddenly, something in me shouted, *NO!* I remembered the rubber band and made my decision: I would not shrink the vision. Instead, I would stretch reality to meet it. The consultant didn't get the job, so you now have the full book.

When You Feel Like Quitting

With Legacy Projects, there will be moments, sometimes entire weeks, when you feel like you've had enough. You'll think, "Why did I start this?" You'll hear a voice whisper, "You're too late." You'll feel the weight of the distance between where you are and where you thought you'd be by now.

There was a moment during this book's creation when I nearly quit. Doubt crept in, and the idea of a smaller, simpler project seemed tempting. But I paused, reflected on the original vision, and remembered why I began. The conversations, the pages already written, and the sense of purpose reignited my resolve.

It's common to hit an emotional fog during big projects—what researchers call the "messy middle." This discomfort signals you're nearing your goal, not failing. If the journey were easy, it wouldn't matter as much. Building a Legacy Project is like planting an oak tree; it takes time to grow, but its impact lasts. You're not just finishing a project. You're creating something enduring.

Now let's look at another mindset that will help you through the messy middle of the project....

The Gap and the Gain: Measure from Where You Started

In *The Gap and the Gain*, Dr. Benjamin Hardy and Dan Sullivan introduce a transformative mindset shift that every Power Project™ creator needs.

Here's the core idea:

- **The Gap** is what you feel when you measure yourself against your ideal.
- **The Gain** is what you feel when you measure yourself against your starting point.

Living in the Gap makes progress hard to see by keeping you focused only on what's left to achieve. In contrast, living in the Gain means measuring how far you've come, which sparks gratitude and motivation.

When I shifted from the Gap to the Gain, I regained perspective and remembered why I started. You'll need this reminder too, especially during challenging moments in big projects.

Ask yourself: Am I viewing my journey through the Gap or the Gain? If you're feeling discouraged, try looking back at what you've achieved. Even small steps count. Let them remind you how much you've grown and that your journey is just beginning.

How to Live in the Gain

1. **Reflect daily.**
   At the end of each day, ask: *"What progress did I make today?"*
2. **Track your wins.**
   Keep a running list of small and large victories.

(It's hard to feel defeated when you're surrounded by proof of progress.)

3. **Set benchmarks based on your starting point, not someone else's finish line.**
   Success is relative to your growth, not someone else's highlight reel.

4. **Celebrate milestones.**
   Don't wait for the finish line to celebrate. Throw a party at mile marker 3.

5. **Reframe the hard days.**
   Even setbacks can be gains—if you learn from them.

Having a project keeps you anchored in the present, drawing your focus away from worries or regrets. When you're actively engaged—building, writing, or organizing— you enter a state of flow, where focus and enjoyment come naturally. This immersion brings renewed energy, motivation, and a quiet sense of joy to your daily routine.

How to Choose Your Next Project

The beauty of projects is their infinite variety. The right project for you is one that aligns with your interests, values, and circumstances.

Here are some simple prompts to help you discover your next project:

- **What excites me?** What topic, skill, or goal sparks my curiosity or enthusiasm?

- **What legacy do I want to leave?** What contribution would I like to make for my family, community, or future generations?
- **What problem can I solve?** Is there a challenge around me that I feel motivated to tackle?
- **What dream have I delayed?** Is there something I've always wanted to do but put off until "someday"?

Answer these questions honestly, and you'll have a list of project ideas ready to pursue. So, let's make this personal. What will your next project be?

The Final Word from Larry

Yes, Larry Walters launched himself into the sky with a lawn chair and some helium. Yes, he ultimately disrupted air traffic and knocked out power. Yes, it was reckless. But when asked why, he did give us an answer worth remembering: *A man can't just sit around.*

And you weren't made to sit around, either. Not here. Not now. Not in the second half of your one wild and precious life. So, grab a notebook or open a document right now. Write down three possible Power Projects™ that spark your interest. Circle one. Commit to a first step, no matter how small. Because once you commit, you'll feel the surge of momentum.

Power Projects™ are your secret weapon, infusing your days with meaning while keeping your mind and spirit alive. Pick up the hammer, the pen, the paintbrush, the shovel, the phone—whatever your tool may be. Your days will brighten, and your energy will rise, and your purpose will move from concept to action.

Project Type	Description	Examples
Momentum Project (Short Timeline)	Quick wins. Complete in a few hours, a day, or a week. Builds momentum.	Plant a flower bed, write a legacy letter, host a dinner.
Quarterly Project (90-Day Focus)	Substantial project to be completed in approximately 90 days. Creates focus and rhythm.	Mentor a teen, start a podcast, build a garden shed.
Legacy Project (Long-Term Vision)	Major effort—may take a year or more. Deeply meaningful, long-term legacy.	Write a book, launch a nonprofit, preserve family history.

Prompt	Your Reflection
What is your bold vision for this project?	
Where is your current reality in comparison?	

✎ Activation Spotlight

Don't Just Burn the Old Map. Draw One Ten Times Bigger

After redefining what reinvention means, here's something surprising that will challenge how you think about your next chapter in life: *10x is Easier Than 2x*. That's the counterintuitive message from Dr. Benjamin Hardy and Dan Sullivan's book, and it has everything to do with the second half of life.

When you aim for 2x, you're still operating within your current framework. You keep most of your habits, commitments, routines—even parts of your identity that may no longer fit. You're tweaking the old map.

But going 10x? That requires a new map entirely. To go 10x, you can't carry everything forward. You must focus on the 20% of your life—your skills, relationships, and passions—that generate 80% of your momentum, joy, and impact. The rest? You release it.

And here's the paradox: when you focus only on what truly matters, you stop wasting energy on what doesn't. Life gets lighter, not heavier. Your path becomes clearer, and you move faster with less friction.

Going 10x is easier because it's aligned and focused. So don't play small out of habit. If something inside you is stirring—if your vision for this next season feels bigger than your current life—listen to it.

What if your second half of life isn't about scaling back, but about finally going all in?

What would 10x look like for you? Not necessarily more effort. Just more alignment, focus, and courage.

PART IV
PRACTICE

Great lives aren't built on big moments.
They're built on small daily moves.

CHAPTER 13

LIFE HACKS FOR NEVER RETIRE LIVING

*"Knowledge is of no value unless you
put it into practice."*
—Anton Chekhov

The Wisdom of Simplicity

Simple things hold quiet brilliance. A handwritten note, a timely walk, a hearty laugh. These aren't just pleasant actions; they create structure, spark joy, and propel us forward. They keep us present while guiding us toward our potential.

This chapter contains numerous practical strategies that can significantly enhance your energy, relationships, health, and momentum. Though these strategies may appear minor at first glance, their effectiveness becomes evident with consistent practice. They represent the types of daily disciplines and nuanced adjustments that, over time, cultivate a life characterized by joy, intentionality, and profound fulfillment.

Read each one carefully, and ask yourself: *Am I applying this? Could this fit into my weekly routine? What would change if I practiced this intentionally?*

You don't need numerous strategies to transform your life—just a few effective ones that you practice regularly. Let's begin....

Hack #1: Start Before You're Ready
Momentum creates clarity. Action builds confidence.

Many people in their second half wait for clarity, confidence, and perfect timing, but what they need is momentum. You gain clarity and confidence by starting. Whether launching a business, writing a book, starting a fitness habit, or engaging in meaningful work, begin with a small step without overthinking or overplanning.

Challenge Prompt:
What's something you've been waiting to start because you didn't feel "ready"?
Write one small action you'll take this week to start anyway.

Hack #2: View Problems Through a New Lens

Feeling overwhelmed often happens when we blend all our problems into one emotional wave, making us feel like we're drowning. I found relief in a quote: *Problems always come in single file.*

This perspective helps us realize that although multiple challenges may loom, we can only solve them one at a time. Even the toughest times come moment by moment. Nobody can handle everything at once, but you can tackle the next problem in front of you.

This mindset is grounding and keeps you calm and focused. Instead of saying, "I'm drowning in problems!" say, "Here's the one I need to deal with now. The rest can wait." Picture your problems lined up at your door—tackle each as it comes, one at a time.

Challenge Prompt
What's the problem in front of me right now? That's my focus.

Hack #3: Spend It While It Matters
Money is worthless if you don't use it to live.

Most people don't think about it, but money has a shelf life. It's not just about saving it. It's about using it while it still matters. I once heard someone say, "If I want to go heli-skiing, it's not going to happen when I'm 89."

Use your money wisely and in a timely manner, while you can enjoy it. Wait too long, and you'll have only numbers and regrets.

The real return on investment isn't just financial—it's the experiences, relationships, growth, and impact that money enables when used wisely. It's also the contributions you make as you give generously, with a cheerful heart. So, don't hoard your opportunities. Spend your resources strategically, while you still have the health, energy, and relationships to enjoy them.

Challenge Prompt:

Where have you been hoarding your resources?
How might you begin using your time and money more appropriately?

Hack #4: Track Small Wins

Progress you can see is progress you will keep.

We all want momentum, but most of us wait to feel motivated before we act. Here's the truth: action creates motivation, not the other way around. Tracking small wins is one of the most powerful ways to create momentum, as it allows you to see your progress. And that changes everything.

Several years ago, I made a commitment to a simple daily exercise routine. To keep myself going, I used a physical calendar. Every day I completed my workout, I marked a big red X on that day. The first week, it was just a few scattered marks. Then came a string. Then a longer one. Suddenly, that calendar became more than a tracker. It was a visual chain of discipline and victory.

And I adopted a simple rule: *Don't break the chain.* The X's proved I was making progress. And each day I succeeded, it got easier to show up the next day. I didn't want to lose the streak.

Was I perfect? No. Did I miss a day? Of course. But here's the key: just go back to it the next day. Think of it like brushing or flossing your teeth. If you miss once, you don't give up on dental hygiene forever. You just brush or floss the next day. The chain is about consistency, not perfection.

Why This Works: The Science of Tracking

Psychologists call this the *Goal Gradient Effect*. It describes how our motivation intensifies as we get closer to a goal. Classic behavior experiments with rats and modern studies with human loyalty programs both demonstrate that proximity to a desired outcome naturally boosts effort.

This happens because tracking progress activates the brain's reward system—dopamine primes us for action, builds momentum, reinforces identity, and helps prevent overwhelm.

In practical terms: When you can see that you're closer to a goal, each step forward becomes more energizing, and quitting feels harder. That's the neuroscience of finishing what you started.

James Clear, author of *Atomic Habits*, explains it this way: "Every action you take is a vote for the type of person you want to become." The small Xs? They're daily votes.

You can track almost anything. The key is to keep it simple, doable, and visible.

- Exercise or steps walked
- Water intake
- Time spent reading or learning
- Social outreach (texts, calls, notes sent)
- Writing, journaling, or creative work
- Spiritual disciplines (prayer, reading, gratitude)
- Sleep hours or screen-free evenings

You don't need an app (though those work too). A wall calendar, a bullet journal, or a sheet of paper will do. The magic is in the daily check-in. Life happens. But here's the 3-step mindset shift:

1. Don't break the chain twice in a row.
2. Don't turn a miss into a meltdown.
3. Don't shame yourself—just reset and move forward.

Challenge Prompt:
What will you begin tracking this week?
Identify one thing, then grab a calendar and start your chain today.

Hack #5: Change Your Environment, Change Your Life
Don't wait for motivation. Surround yourself with it.

When my friend Steve went in for his routine physical ten years ago, he wasn't expecting a wake-up call. But that's exactly what he got.

At the time, Steve was 35 pounds overweight, burned out from long hours at a high-pressure job, and getting zero exercise. His doctor didn't sugarcoat it: "You are a prime candidate for either a stroke or a heart attack. If you change nothing, I'll be seeing you again soon—but it will be in the emergency room."

She didn't hand him a fitness plan. She gave him a simple challenge: "Pick anything that gets you moving—and commit to it for life." Rather than prescribing a program, she wisely recommended a pattern.

Steve hated running. But he bought a pair of shoes and told himself, "I can tolerate 30 minutes a day." The first few weeks were miserable. But then came a subtle shift. One month in, he didn't hate it so much. Soon after, he signed up for a local 5K. Then a 10K. Then he joined a local running club, and that was the beginning of a breakthrough.

One day, one of the runners said casually, "You'll be doing a marathon soon." Steve laughed it off. "No way. Not interested." But something had already started to change. Simply by being in a group of people who ran marathons, his internal thermostat started to rise. He didn't force it. He absorbed it. Soon came a half-marathon. After that, a complete one. Today, Steve has completed marathons in multiple states.

What began as a doctor's warning turned into a new identity—not because he found a new goal, but because he found a new environment. Just being with people who ran marathons changed him. It wasn't a motivational speech or a twelve-step program. It was exposure. Osmosis. He was rising to the level of the room.

Science confirms we're wired for *social mirroring*—we unconsciously adopt the habits, standards, and energy of those we surround ourselves with. Whether it's your pace of life, your health routines, or your mindset, you are becoming more like your environment every day.

Your environment is either pulling you forward or holding you back. Change your environment, and you change your trajectory. Want to grow? Get around growers. Want to run? Join up with runners. Want to write a book? Spend time with authors. Want to reinvent yourself? Start hanging out with people who already have.

Challenge Prompt:
Who are the three people or environments you spend the most time in? Are they lifting your vision—or limiting it?
Take one bold step to upgrade your environment this week. Sign up for a club. Join a group. Attend an event. Meet someone new who is doing what you desire.

Hack #6: Embrace Technology (without letting it overwhelm you)
A Mindset Shift: From Intimidation to Empowerment

Technology can sometimes feel like trying to sip from a firehose. The moment you master one app, five new ones hit the market. QR codes, smart homes, chatbots, virtual meetings… It's easy to throw your hands up and say, "This just isn't for me." But here's the truth: technology isn't the enemy. Confusion is.

Think of technology as a menu, not a mandate. You're not expected to order everything. Just pick what works for your life, your goals, and your interests. Use it as a tool, not a tyrant. You don't need to understand *how* it all works. You just need to ask, "Would this make my life better or easier?"

Studies show that older adults who stay digitally connected experience less depression, better memory, and increased life satisfaction. And guess what? Younger generations love to help. Ask a younger family member or neighbor to show you how something works—it builds a bridge in both directions.

Challenge Prompt:
Which technology have you been avoiding that could be beneficial?
Choose one and set a learning goal this week.

Hack #7: Embrace AI—Your New Everyday Ally
Don't fear the future. Invite it in.

Artificial Intelligence (AI) is no longer a concept of the future; it's a practical tool that's enhancing daily life in countless ways. For those of us above 50, embracing AI can open doors to new experiences, streamline daily tasks, and even spark creativity. Think of it like having a helpful assistant—except this one never sleeps, doesn't judge, and can help with just about anything.

One of the most user-friendly tools available today is ChatGPT, a free-to-use AI that can assist, inspire, and energize your day in more ways than you might imagine. You don't have to be "techy" to use it. You just need to stay curious.

To begin your AI journey, visit chat.openai.com. Click "Sign Up" and create a free account. Once inside, you're greeted by a simple chat window.

Interesting & Everyday Ways to Use ChatGPT

- **Meal Planning**: List the ingredients in your fridge and get fresh recipe ideas in seconds.
- **Travel Planning**: Create day-by-day itineraries for your next road trip or overseas adventure.
- **Learning Made Simple**: Ask it to explain a complicated topic (like Bitcoin, cholesterol, or the Electoral College) in plain English.
- **Writing Help**: Draft emails, letters, social media posts, thank-you notes—or even a poem for your grandchild.
- **Home Projects**: Get a step-by-step guide for cleaning gutters, planting fall vegetables, or organizing your garage.
- **Creative Inspiration**: Generate a list of fun date night ideas, unique birthday gifts, or conversation starters for family dinners.

- **Legacy Projects**: Use ChatGPT to organize your life stories into chapters for a family memoir or gratitude journal.
- **Book Summaries**: Don't have time to read a 300-page bestseller? Ask ChatGPT to summarize it in a few key takeaways.

Challenge Prompt:
If you haven't already, open a free ChatGPT account this week. Type in a simple prompt like: "Give me 5 ideas for organizing my closet," or "Help me write a thoughtful birthday message." You have wisdom. AI brings speed. Together? That's powerful.

Hack #8: A Body in Motion Stays...Alive

You've probably heard Newton's First Law of Motion: *An object at rest stays at rest, and an object in motion stays in motion...unless acted upon by an outside force.* Newton was talking about physics, but he might as well have been talking about aging.

A body at rest—sitting in a recliner, watching TV, avoiding movement—starts to stay at rest. Muscles weaken, joints stiffen, and energy fades. The less we move, the harder it becomes to move.

A body in motion tends to remain in motion. Regular movement can contribute to sustained strength, mobility, and energy over time. Maintaining physical activity as we age supports overall health. And movement relates not only to fitness but also to maintaining independence.

- **Walk daily.** Not because it burns calories, but because it keeps you upright.
- **Lift things.** Not to impress anyone, but so you can lift your own groceries at 90.
- **Stretch.** Not to become a gymnast, but to keep tying your own shoes.
- **Stay engaged.** Not just physically, but mentally and socially. Motion in the body starts with motion in the mind.

Retirement should be the season of more movement, not less. More adventures, not more sitting. More purpose, not more passivity. Because in the end, the real "outside force" that keeps us going isn't gravity. It's having something worth moving toward.

Challenge Prompt:
Write down three things you could do daily to move more. Choose one and get started today.

Hack #9: Keep Your WITTS™
When people ask, "What do you do?" Tell them, "Whatever it takes."

While there is a ton of wisdom and strategy throughout this chapter, none of it will bring lasting results without one key ingredient: commitment. Deep, unwavering, all-in commitment. That's the power behind the mindset of *WITTS—Whatever It Takes to Succeed™*.

One vivid example of this comes from Tom Fatjo, as shared in his book, *With No Fear of Failure*. Tom didn't set out to build a national waste management company. He just wanted to improve things in his own neighborhood. So, he bought a single garbage truck and got to work. Early on, he made a commitment: "I will do whatever it takes to make this business a success." For Tom, that meant that no job was beneath him, no obstacle too discouraging, and no challenge too dirty.

In the early days, before going national, Tom drove the truck and collected the garbage. One early morning, when the compression mechanism failed, Tom found himself in the back of the garbage truck, manually stomping down the trash with his hands and feet. Though frustrated, he still managed to mutter the words that were shaping his journey: "So this is what it takes!"

That's the essence of WITTS™. It's a mindset that refuses to be stopped by inconvenience, doubt, or discomfort. It means you show up with grit, with purpose, and with the willingness to pay the price required to finish what you started.

Let that be your approach to the hacks, tools, and strategies in this book. Don't skim them and don't dabble. Find a couple that work for you and then do whatever it takes to succeed. WITTS™: It's not just an acronym. It's a declaration.

Challenge Prompt:
What project is so meaningful that you will fully commit to completing it?
What areas of the project will require a WITTS™ mindset?

Now, Activate the Hacks

You've just explored a toolkit of practical, mindset-shifting, soul-fueling hacks—each one designed to help you live with purpose, energy, and joy in the second half of life. But reading them isn't enough. Now it's time to activate!

Pick one. Just one. Don't wait for the perfect moment. Start today. Start messy. Start small. But start. Because the life you want isn't built in big leaps. It's built in daily choices. These hacks are your tools. Your habits are the blueprint. Your action is the spark. Small things done consistently will eventually create huge, satisfying results.

CHAPTER 14

FROM DRIFT TO DRIVE: WHY YOUR SCHEDULE STILL MATTERS

"Don't squander time, for that's the stuff life is made of."
—Benjamin Franklin

J.K. Rowling, now the bestselling author of the 21st century, didn't begin her journey with fame, wealth, or ideal conditions. In fact, when she began writing *Harry Potter*, her life was at its lowest point. She was a single mother living in Edinburgh, recently divorced, jobless, and living on government assistance. Struggling with depression, she described herself at the time as being "as poor as it is possible to be in modern Britain without being homeless."

But even in that dark and difficult season, she made a firm decision: she would write. Not someday. Not when life got easier. She would write now, and she would schedule it. With her infant daughter asleep in a stroller beside her, Rowling would find quiet corners of cafés and carve out time to work on the story she believed in. It wasn't glamorous, but it was consistent.

She didn't wait for inspiration to strike. She set a rhythm, blocked out time, however fragmented, and kept showing up.

The manuscript for *Harry Potter* was rejected by twelve different publishers before finally being accepted by Bloomsbury. Even then, she was told not to expect much success because fantasy books for children didn't sell. But she had already learned something far more important than market predictions: when your dream has a schedule, it has a future.

She wrote through poverty, through discouragement, and through rejection. Her goal had structure, and her vision had a place in her calendar. As a result, her pages became chapters, her chapters became a manuscript, and her manuscript became a movement that would touch the world.

J.K. Rowling's story reminds us that the schedule isn't just about efficiency. It's about becoming the kind of person who shows up, even when life is hard. It's about turning ordinary minutes into extraordinary impact. And here's the deeper truth: the principles in this book—reflection, reinvention, contribution, connection—they don't just sound good. They only become real when you schedule them.

Why You Need a Schedule

There's a hidden truth few people realize about traditional retirement: the calendar doesn't disappear—it just stops getting filled. And when our days go unstructured, so do our lives. We lose our rhythm, forget our why, and purpose slowly slips into passivity.

A *Never Retire* life isn't something that appears out of nowhere. It's something you design, and design begins with a calendar. Your schedule is your declaration that your life still matters and that your time is still valuable. That you still have people to bless, gifts to give, and something worth waking up for every day.

Scheduling becomes not a cage, but a canvas—a framework for freedom, and a structure that gives shape to significance.

Why Time Feels Faster as We Age

Time is one of the most fascinating, and misunderstood realities we experience. It's invisible, yet it shapes everything. We often say, "I don't have enough time," when the truth is, we all have the same amount. What we do with it— that's where the difference lies.

As we age, time doesn't just pass—it accelerates. Not because the days have changed, but because our perception has. Psychologists explain this through the *proportional theory of time*: to a 10-year-old, one year is 10% of life lived; to a 70-year-old, it's just over 1%. The older we get, the smaller each year feels in the grand scope of life, making months fly and years blur.

If we're not careful, unstructured time becomes lost time. Days blur, weeks vanish, and we eventually look back and ask, "Where did it all go?" That's why scheduling matters. A schedule is a container. Without it, time leaks away.

There's a principle from British author and historian C. Northcote Parkinson, who observed this truth: *Work expands to fill the time available for its completion.* This idea, now known as *Parkinson's Law*, applies not just to work, but to life. When time is left open and undefined, tasks, distractions, and even laziness will rush in to fill the space. But when you block your time with purpose, you control the flow.

Time is one of the few things we cannot earn more of. We can't manufacture it, slow it down, or stockpile it. That's why the schedule is sacred. It is how we honor the fleeting, finite gift of time.

Your Personal Morning Routine

Now, let's talk about the morning. What is your daily routine? Is it serving you well?

> You schedule what matters. If nothing is scheduled, you're saying nothing matters.

I personally wake up before 5 a.m. most days. Not because I'm trying to impress anyone or wanting to join the 5 AM Club, but because I know how much better I function with rhythm and structure. A morning routine doesn't make you rigid. It makes you ready. It gives your mind and spirit a foundation before the chaos of the world demands your attention.

A Good Morning Begins the Night Before

If you want to take control of your day, your mindset, and your energy, don't wait until the alarm clock goes off. Start preparing the night before with these simple habits:

- **Shut off technology early.** Research shows that blue light interferes with your melatonin production and tricks your brain into thinking it's still daytime.
- **Get a full night of quality sleep.** Sleep isn't just rest—it's repair. It's when your brain processes memories, your body recharges, and your emotional system recalibrates. No routine matters if you're constantly running on empty.
- **Know your top 1–2 priorities before your head hits the pillow.** Don't wake up and start your day by asking, "What do I need to do today?" Decide the night before. When you wake up with a plan, you step into your day with purpose instead of passivity.

Start the Day Right: Make Your Bed

Yes, really. And not just because your mom told you to. It might seem trivial, but making your bed is one of the most powerful ways to start your day. It's like the first domino—

it knocks the others into place. You begin with order and claim your first win of the day.

In his now-famous commencement address at the University of Texas, Admiral William H. McRaven—Navy SEAL and four-star admiral—shared this advice with graduating students: "If you want to change the world, start by making your bed." That single quote launched a global movement and a bestselling book.

"If you make your bed every morning, you will have accomplished the first task of the day... And if by chance you have a miserable day, you will come home to a bed that is made— that you made—and a made bed gives you encouragement that tomorrow will be better."—Admiral William H. McRaven, *Make Your Bed*

Engage in Stillness
Prayer, meditation, reflection. Give your mind space before the day begins to crowd in. It anchors your heart for the day ahead.

Journal and Read Something Inspirational

When journaling, you don't need to write pages. Just jot down what you're grateful for, what you're aiming for today, or what you're noticing in your life. This builds self-awareness and focus.

Also, start your mind with something uplifting, wise, or energizing. For me, that includes daily time in Scripture.

Skip the news headlines or social media scroll and choose something that nourishes your spirit. Just a few pages can make a difference.

Having a morning schedule is not about being rigid or inflexible. It's about giving your day direction before the noise of the world starts dictating it for you.

What's currently disrupting your mornings? (Late nights? Distractions? No routine?)

What's one thing you could change tonight to create a better tomorrow morning?

Design your own ideal 30-minute morning routine. What would it include?

Time Blocking: The Power of Pre-Decided Time

Here's one of the most powerful scheduling tools I've ever used: Time Blocking. This means that instead of keeping a vague to-do list, you pre-decide when you'll do your most meaningful work, and assign it a firm spot in your calendar. No negotiations. No multitasking.

The brilliance of time blocking is that it protects what matters most. When distractions or urges arise (and they always do), you don't need willpower to resist. You just say, "Sorry, this time is already spoken for." And that can include time with a close friend or family member. And, of course, time scheduled for yourself.

Cal Newport, author of *Deep Work*, built his career on time blocking. He schedules each hour of his workday, not because he's obsessed with control, but because he's obsessed with focus. He says: "The key to time management is to see your day as a collection of blocks, not open space. That shift changes everything."

Studies show that people who block their time are significantly more productive and experience greater mental clarity and calm. Why? Because they've reduced decision fatigue. Their brain isn't scrambling to decide what to do next, because it's already decided.

The White Space Principle

In publishing, white space isn't empty—it's what makes the words readable. In life, it's what makes the moments meaningful. Don't cram your schedule edge to edge. Build in margins. Create pause.

White space is where creativity awakens, clarity returns, and renewal begins. It's not wasted time. It's where your next idea, insight, or second wind often finds you.

The Weekly Rhythm of the Never Retire Life

When you're time blocking, it's helpful to create a weekly framework with time slots blocked off for the entire seven days. That way you have a picture of what your week will look like. Try structuring your week in broad rhythms, not micromanaged minutes. When you look at your week this way, you will feel balanced rather than behind.

- **Growth Time** – reading, learning, skill-building
- **Connection Time** – family, friends, intergenerational impact
- **Contribution Time** – volunteering, mentoring, legacy projects
- **Adventure Time** – travel, spontaneity, trying new things
- **Rest and Reflection** – Meditation, prayer, silence, nature walk

Living to Age 156 – How to Expand the Horizon of Time

Here's where it gets radical. Dan Sullivan's book *My Plan for Living to 156* presents a powerful yet simple idea: the number you believe represents your lifespan shapes how you live. Most people unconsciously set this number based on family history, genetics, or societal averages—locking themselves into an expiration date.

But Dan asks his clients to imagine living to age 156. Not because he expects them to, but because he wants to stretch their mental framework. Dan realized that when people reach midlife—and especially as they move beyond it—they often subconsciously shrink their vision. They

155

begin to scale back their ambitions and express sentiments such as: *It's too late to embark on a new endeavor. I won't have time to finish. My best years are behind me.*

But what if you assumed you had more time than you think? What if you approached life not as a short sprint to the end, but as a marathon still unfolding? What if you began to live and plan as if you were going to be 100, 110, 120—or even 156?

Even if you don't get there, the perspective is what matters. Because when you expand the horizon of time, you expand your courage, creativity, and willingness to invest in your future. You start making long-term decisions, not short-term compromises. You stay open to reinvention. You take care of your health not just for today, but for the decades to come. You think bigger, dream larger, and live fuller. And most of all, you enjoy the process, because you stop racing against the clock and start embracing the journey.

So, ask yourself: *If I believed I had another 50 years, how differently would I live today?*

Always Schedule What Matters

The main takeaway from this chapter: If something matters, schedule it.

While it sounds simple, you've learned that it's one of the most powerful strategies you can use in the second half of life. We all start with good intentions—to connect with friends, to exercise, to start that project, to write that handwritten note. But the truth is, good intentions without a system quickly fade into forgotten wishes.

Your calendar isn't just a list of appointments—it's your commitment device. It's where dreams get scheduled, and goals become reality. And this isn't just motivational fluff. Psychologists call it *implementation intention*: the act of deciding in advance when and where you'll do something.

Research shows this simple habit can boost your odds of follow-through by up to 91%.

Don't leave important things floating in your mind, hoping they'll find time. Give them a place in your day. If you want to send a card, schedule it. If you want to call a friend, block the time. If you want to exercise, write it in the calendar. If you want to work on your second-half reinvention, give it protected time.

When you look back on your week, your calendar will tell the truth of your priorities. When your day has a rhythm, your mind has room to create. Your energy is conserved because you're not constantly deciding what to do next. You've already decided. That's the hidden power of routine.

What's one thing you care about that isn't on your calendar yet?

Block 15 minutes this week for a small but meaningful action, and then keep the appointment with yourself.

CHAPTER 15

PRACTICES THAT STRENGTHEN CONNECTION & COMMUNITY

"If you want to go fast, go alone.
If you want to go far, go together."
—African Proverb

The Secret Beneath the Surface

In Northern California stand some of the tallest and oldest living organisms on Earth—the mighty redwoods and giant sequoias. Some of these trees that stretch over 350 feet into the sky have lived for more than 2,000 years.

At first glance, you might assume their strength comes from deep roots plunging far into the earth. But that's not the case. In fact, their roots are surprisingly shallow—some only 5 feet deep. So, how have they stood for millennia through storms, droughts, fires, and earthquakes? The secret lies in something invisible and underground: proximity and connection. They are strong because of the connection they have with each other.

Redwoods don't grow in isolation. They grow in groves. And beneath the surface, their roots intertwine with the roots of other trees nearby. They literally hold each other up. Their strength is not in solitary depth, but in relational width. Alone, a redwood would likely tumble. Together, they rise and endure.

That, in a single image, is the message of this chapter. You and I were not made to do life alone. We were not designed to stand through the storms of aging, loss, reinvention, and transition with a shallow root system and no support. If we want to live long, strong, meaningful lives—lives that last— we must grow together. We need relationships, community, and proximity. In short, we need people!

This chapter offers you a set of *Connection Moves*— simple but powerful practices that strengthen your relationships, deepen your sense of belonging, and expand your legacy. Let's learn from the redwoods how to stand strong—together.

Connection Move #1: Relationships Keep You Alive (Literally)

Because connection is not a luxury. It's a lifeline.

> If your soul feels tired, you might not need a vacation. You might just need a good conversation.

In the second half of life, many people focus on finances, health, or leaving a legacy. All important. But one factor quietly shapes your well-being more than almost anything else: your relationships. Not just how many, but how deep. Not how busy, but how intentional.

Study after study confirms it: strong, healthy relationships are one of the most powerful predictors of well-being. People with close connections live longer, feel happier, recover faster from illness, and are less likely to suffer cognitive decline.

The Harvard Study of Adult Development—an 80+ year research project—put it best: "Good relationships keep us happier and healthier. Period."

Loneliness, on the other hand, has been found to be as damaging as smoking 15 cigarettes a day. And yet many in their 50s, 60s, and beyond quietly drift into isolation—especially after retirement, relocation, or loss.

Think about relationships like fuel. Some fill you up while others drain you. You don't need hundreds of connections. Just a few that matter. The key is to invest in the ones that refill your tank—people who listen, laugh, challenge you, and remind you of who you are. And then, be that person for someone else.

You don't drift into meaningful relationships. You build them with intention, time, and presence. Learn to pause during busy days and ask: "Who haven't I connected with in a while?" Then send a message, make a call, or invite someone for coffee. It doesn't have to be long or deep. Sometimes it's just a "thinking of you" text or a short handwritten note.

Those small touches of connection often turn into the best part of someone's day. Because in the end, we don't just need each other. We fuel each other.

Connection Move Reflection:
Who in your life makes you feel seen and known?
And who needs that from you this week?

Connection Move #2: Leave People Better Than You Found Them
"People will forget what you said, forget what you did, but never forget how you made them feel."—Maya Angelou

We live in a world obsessed with resumes, titles, and accomplishments. But at the end of the day, most people won't remember what you built, achieved, or posted online. They'll remember how you made them feel. That's why this Connection Move may be the most powerful of all.

Here's something I try to practice when I'm at an event, church, or even a casual gathering: I ask myself one quiet but powerful question: *Who might need my help—or my encouragement—right now?*

> "Life is what we make it. Always has been, always will be."
> —Grandma Moses

Then I look around and let my heart lead. And once I sense that person, I make a conscious effort to focus totally on them, without distraction. Not rushing off to the next thing. Not glancing at my phone. Just being there. Sometimes it's a conversation, a simple compliment, or a listening ear. At other times, it's just sitting with someone and letting them know they're seen.

This one small shift has changed the way I engage with people. It's changed how I leave a room—and how people feel when I do. There's a reason the old saying still holds true: *People don't care how much you know until they know how much you care.*

Genuine care is rare. But when people feel it, they never forget it. You don't need to fix their life. You don't need to say something brilliant. You just need to show up—and care!

> A handwritten note feels sacred. It communicates to the one receiving it: "You matter enough for me to pause. To write. To send."

The Psychology of Being Seen

One of the deepest human needs is to be seen, heard, and valued. Psychologist Carl Rogers called it *unconditional positive regard*—a sense that you are accepted just as you are. When you focus on others with genuine compassion, you create emotional safety, raise their self-worth, and invite honesty. And the ripple effect? It goes further than you'll ever know.

You don't need a stage or spotlight—just presence, intentionality, and love. So, the next time you're in a meeting or even standing in line, pause, look around, and focus on who might be carrying something heavy. Then approach, smile, and say something kind, or just be available. Your words and your presence might be the very thing that gets them through the day.

Connection Prompt:
Who could you intentionally lift this week?
Write their name and one way you'll do it.

Connection Move #3: Laugh More. The World Needs It.
The best medicine doesn't come in a bottle. It starts with a chuckle.

Laughter is one of life's most underrated superpowers. It boosts your immune system, relaxes your muscles, improves circulation, lowers stress hormones, and releases endorphins—your body's natural feel-good chemicals.

And it doesn't just change your body. It changes your mindset, and often the mindset of others as well. A good laugh can reset your perspective, soften your stress, and remind you that joy is still possible—even in difficult times.

The Airport Incident

A few years ago, I was passing time during a long layover in Florida. You know the drill. Hurry up and wait. So I did what many people do: I grabbed a cup of coffee, found a spot near a busy terminal, and started people-watching. (Free entertainment if you know how to do it right.)

Across the terminal, I noticed a woman hurrying along with several shopping bags when one slipped from her hands. Then another. In the scramble, a toy she'd bought— *Laughing Louie*, the red clown that laughs hysterically when pressed—fell to the ground. It started cackling like a maniac, echoing throughout the terminal. And as she quickly gathered her things, that ridiculous clown wouldn't stop laughing, as if mocking her entire predicament.

In one of the best comic timing moments I've ever witnessed, she finally looked at it, exasperated, and literally shouted, "SHUT UP!"

I nearly spit out my coffee, and others also let out a laugh. Before it was over, she herself was smiling, evidently seeing the humor in a situation where stress had tried to take over.

Humor is like that. It sneaks in when you least expect it and lightens the load. It doesn't hide, but you do have to train your eyes and ears to see it. And laughter isn't just about entertainment. It's about perspective, reminding you this moment will pass. This tension isn't final, and the mistake will make a great story one day.

You don't have to chase laughter—just be open to it. Train your eyes and ears to pick up on life's little absurdities. Humor is everywhere, but most people are too distracted or stressed to notice.

Remember to smile more often and laugh at yourself a little more. And when something goes wrong, pause and ask, *"Will this be funny later?"* (It usually will.)

Connection Prompt:
What makes you laugh?
How can you bring more of that into your week and into the lives of others?

Connection Move #4: Mend the Fence While You Can
One of the most powerful connections you can make in life is the one you restore.

When I was in my mid-twenties, I confided in an older man named Harley—a wise and trusted friend from Arkansas. I was carrying frustration about a strained relationship with a close family member. I explained the history, the drama, and my desire to help this person to see more clearly so we could mend our relationship.

When I finished explaining the situation, I anticipated that Harley would offer some great advice—maybe a script to follow or some relational tactics. Instead, he asked me a question that made me wonder if he was even listening.

"Bob, do you know anything about car engines?" Wondering where this was going, I let him know I didn't know much. He then launched into a short lesson about pistons, metal parts, and friction. Though I wasn't asking for a mini course on combustion engines, Harley continued, "Anytime you have metal parts working that closely together, there will be friction. That's why we add oil to an engine."

Then he paused, looked me in the eye, and said words I'll never forget: "Love is the oil." That was it. Not another

166

word from Harley. He never elaborated, and he didn't have to. I got the point.

I sat there in silence for a while, reflecting on the simple, powerful lesson I had just learned. In close relationships—siblings, spouses, old friends—there will be friction. Expect it, but don't leave it unaddressed. Apply the oil. It might be a phone call, a text, a quiet act of kindness, or even an apology. It's never too late, and the power of love to restore is greater than we realize.

Connection Prompt:
Who do you need to extend love toward today?
Where might oil be needed in one of your relationships?

Connection Move #5: Send Handwritten Notes
In the age of overflowing inboxes, text pings, and algorithm-fed feeds, there's one thing that always feels like a breath of fresh air: a handwritten note. It's rare, thoughtful, and profoundly human.

A few years ago, I started one of my favorite habits—sending a handwritten card each week to someone who might need encouragement. Just a note of hope. A reminder that they matter. While I was doing it for others, I started noticing the positive impact this habit was having on me. Neuroscience has a name for this: *Helper's High.* Small acts of kindness activate your brain's reward center, releasing serotonin and dopamine—your body's natural feel-good chemicals.

These cards don't just lift others. They will energize you, boost your well-being, and remind you that kindness is a two-way gift. And if you form this simple habit of mailing a weekly card, you'll hear similar comments: *Your card arrived at exactly the right time. Your note felt like a lifeline. I've saved your handwritten card and have read it again and again.*

The Story that Proves the Point

In some cases, these simple notes will open deeper conversations and build stronger connections than you can imagine.

Helen Mrosla, a teacher in a small Minnesota town, once gave her students a class assignment: write something kind and affirming about each classmate. She compiled the responses and gave each student a list of what their peers said about them.

Years later, one of the students, Mark Eklund, died in military service. After his funeral, his parents showed Helen something folded and worn: the list of affirmations the various students had written to him. The parents said he had carried that list with him ever since her class. Other classmates came forward and said they had saved their lists too. For many, it had become a treasured reminder of their worth.

This is the power of written words. When you send your handwritten note, you may never fully know the impact it will have. But rest assured, it matters deeply.

Make it easy to start:

- Buy a box of cards and stamps.
- Keep them somewhere visible.
- Block out 10 minutes a week to write one.
- Follow the nudge when someone comes to mind.

The trees in California remind us: proximity is strength, and connection is survival. So reach out. Send the note or make the call. Share the laugh. Mend the fence and keep showing up, because the greatest stories from your life won't be about solo success. They'll be about people. Moments of connection and the encouragement you offered. Laughter around the table. Kindness that echoed further than you knew. Don't miss the power of people.

Connection Prompt:
Who could use a handwritten note from you this week?
Send one handwritten card today. Notice how you feel afterward.

✎ Activation Spotlight

It's Not Too Late to Start Something Beautiful

The Art of Following the Spark

Anna didn't pick up a paintbrush until her late seventies. Born in 1860, she lived a quiet life as a farmer's wife in rural New York. She spent her days in rural obscurity, tending fields, raising children, and keeping a humble home. Her evenings were quiet, often spent near a warm fire, embroidering scenes from memory—snowy hillsides, barn dances, children sledding. Nothing she created would ever be shown in a gallery or written about in a magazine. Or so she thought.

In her later years, arthritis eventually forced Anna to give up needlework. Not wanting to sit idle, she searched for something she could still do with her hands. And that's when she found the paintbrush.

With leftover house paint and cheap supplies, she began painting what she knew: rolling hills, horses and buggies, and townsfolk in heavy coats crossing wooden bridges in the snow. Her paintings carried something few others could—warmth, authenticity, and the unfiltered soul of a long, full life.

Eventually, she began selling paintings at the local drugstore for $2 to $3 each. And that might've been the end of the story...until a New York art collector happened to see her work during a stop through town.

He bought every piece. Soon after, she had her first solo exhibition in New York City at age 80.

Suddenly, the art world took notice. She was featured in *Life* and *Time* magazines. Her paintings hung in prestigious galleries. She was honored by President Truman. Hallmark printed her work on greeting cards seen by millions. She painted over 1,500 pieces in her lifetime, and some sold for tens of thousands of dollars. One was later auctioned for $1.2 million.

Her full name was Anna Mary Robertson Moses, but the world would come to know her as Grandma Moses—one of the most beloved American folk artists of the 20th century.

Her story reminds us that:

- It's not too late to start something beautiful.
- You don't need credentials—you need curiosity.
- You don't need a master plan—you need a spark.
- And when that spark is followed by action, it can ignite a legacy.

PART V
PEAK

The summit isn't the end. It's where the view finally makes sense.

CHAPTER 16

THE GREAT PIONEER SPIRIT

*"You can always spot the pioneers by
the arrows in their backs."*
—William H. Calvin

Picture this: It is the early 1800s. Imagine yourself waking up as a pioneer. There's no power grid, no pre-paved roads, no GPS, and no Google Maps.

The sun rises, and you face a land of untamed opportunity. No guarantees await you, and there are no safety nets or government bailouts. All you have is rugged determination, an unshakable vision, and the belief that you can build a better life.

> "All you need for happiness is a good gun, a good horse, and a good wife."
> —Daniel Boone

You gather your tools, build your shelter and grow your food. You look after your family and community. And as the sun sets, you don't measure your success by how easy the day was. You measure by what you built, and by how much closer you are to your goal.

That's the spirit we need to reclaim. The pioneer spirit! Have we forgotten that it literally runs in our blood and is part of our DNA?

The early settlers of America didn't have government systems to bail them out. They didn't build this country by waiting for someone else to pave the road ahead of them. They were the road builders. They didn't wait for rescue. They became the rescuers.

"I have never been lost, but I will admit to being confused for several weeks."
—Daniel Boone

Daniel Boone's words remind us of the pioneer mindset: even when uncertain, you keep moving. You find your way. You create new paths for others to follow. This is the essence of the *Never Retire* movement. It's not merely about continuing to work. It's about continuing to live with purpose, to continue pioneering.

The pioneering spirit declares:

- "I will take ownership of my future."
- "I will carve out my own path, even when it feels uncertain."
- "I will turn obstacles into stepping stones."

The Great Age Shift Has Arrived

We need this pioneering spirit because something monumental is happening right now. A wave is forming beneath the surface of our culture, our economy, and our communities. It's quiet, but it's massive. And by the time most people realize it, it will have already reshaped the world around them. It's the age shift. And it's not coming someday. It's already here.

The demographics in our world are shifting fast. We briefly mentioned some of what is happening near the opening of this book. That alone would be a turning point, but there's more.

According to the U.S. Census Bureau, by 2034—for the first time in American history—there will be more adults over 65 than children under 18.

> "The American Dream can no more remain static than can the American nation... We cannot any longer take an old approach to world problems. They aren't the same problems. It isn't the same world. We must not adopt the methods of our ancestors; instead, we must emulate that pioneer quality in our ancestors that made them attempt new methods for a New World."
> —Eleanor Roosevelt

- By 2030, every Baby Boomer will be at least 65. One in five Americans will be a senior.
- Globally, the population over 65 is expected to more than double, from 761 million in 2021 to over 1.6 billion by 2050.
- Meanwhile, the population of those 85 and older is set to triple in the U.S. by 2060, reaching 19 million.

- Incredibly, by the early 2040s, we may see more people aged 80+ than infants on this planet.

This isn't a distant forecast. It's a reality racing toward us that will bring about a complete reshaping of the human experience. It demands a radical shift in how we view aging, work, purpose, and retirement.

> "Aging is an extraordinary process where you become the person you always should have been."
> —David Bowie

Today? Many people will spend 30+ years in the so-called "retirement phase." And yet, most retirement systems were designed for a time when life expectancy was much shorter, and the "retirement window" was expected to last only a decade or two at best.

This is why the old retirement model is not only outdated—it's dangerous. It leaves millions of capable, experienced, and mission-ready people on the sidelines. It ignores the fact that people are living longer, healthier lives and still want to contribute.

The Retirement Myth

This is the myth many of us have been taught—a subtle but deeply rooted belief that if we work hard enough, follow the rules, and wait our turn, someone else will ensure our well-being in the second half of life. We've been told that governments, systems, institutions, or even corporations will take care of us when we reach "retirement age."

But look around. What we're experiencing is not a rescue. It's a reckoning. The old models are cracking. Social Security systems around the world are under strain. Pensions are evaporating, and health care costs are rising. Life expectancy is increasing—which is good news, but it extends the runway far beyond what most financial plans were built for.

Pioneers of Purpose

Here's the truth that will set you free: No one is coming to save us. That might sound unsettling at first. But listen closely, because it's liberating news. Why? Because it means the power has always been in your hands.

It's time to stop looking for a rescue and start building solutions. It's time to unretire, to create new ventures, and to build new communities. It's time to share your wisdom, to mentor the next generation, to write the book, or to start the project you've delayed. We don't have to wait for rescue.

> "I have written eleven books, but each time I think, 'Uh oh, they're going to find me out now.'"
> —Maya Angelou

We get to build our own rescue boat.

This demographic revolution opens the door for a generation of modern elders to re-engage, to mentor, to start new ventures, to innovate, and to lead. But only if we have the courage to see this moment for what it is: a turning point. Not a slow fade into irrelevance, but a second wind of impact. What was once considered a finish line is now an open frontier.

We get to pioneer new paths, create new solutions, and design a life of purpose, contribution, and vitality. But being a pioneer isn't just about blazing new trails out there. It first starts by winning an internal battle.

The Inner Battle Every Pioneer Faces

Every pioneer faces resistance, but not just from the outside. Some of the fiercest battles are fought in the mind.

One of the most common struggles among those who dare to do something new is *impostor syndrome*—that inner voice that whispers, *"You're not qualified. Who do you think you are to do this?"* Ironically, impostor syndrome shows up precisely when you're growing—stepping into uncharted territory where you've never been before. That's where fear flares up...and where your story begins to unfold.

Research shows that over 70% of people experience impostor syndrome at some point—including some of the most successful leaders, creators, and entrepreneurs on the planet. The difference? They did it anyway! And so can you.

At one point in my own journey, I felt this weight while preparing to step into a new endeavor that stretched me far beyond my comfort zone. I began to second-guess myself, quietly wondering if I was in over my head. That's when I stumbled upon a phrase that stopped me cold:

Everything is Made Up

That one thought changed everything for me. Every system, every process, every organization we admire—someone made it up.

- The **alphabet**? Made up.
- **Skyscrapers**? Made up.
- **Money**? An agreed-upon story.
- **The internet?** Made up by people just figuring it out.
- **Air travel?** Dreamed up by two bicycle mechanics.
- **The calendar?** Invented. And humans still argue over which one to use.

> Everyone is making it up as they go along. Once you realize that everything is made up, you are free to create anything.

Every invention was imagined, drafted, tested, and refined by people who didn't have all the answers—but had the courage to try. That's what pioneers do. They step into the unknown. They create from scratch, and they don't wait for permission. They understand that most of what intimidates us is just someone else's imagination. And we can imagine, too.

You don't need to have everything figured out; you just need to take the next bold step. Remember that just because something hasn't been done by you yet doesn't mean it can't be done. If others have made it up, so can you. That's the beginning of a pioneer's journey.

The Never Retire Declaration

The *Never Retire* mindset isn't just a personal philosophy. It's a necessary response to a global phenomenon. The world needs you now more than ever. The age wave isn't something to fear. It's something to ride. Because age is not the end of relevance, it's the beginning of real leadership.

As pioneers, we boldly declare:
We will not wait for rescue. We are the pioneers of purpose. Realizing that everything is made up, we blaze new trails with faith and confidence. We will not settle for a life of quiet decline. We will live with fire, with focus, and with fierce resolve. No one is coming to save us—and that's the best news of all. Because it means our future is not in someone else's hands but in ours. And that is exactly where it belongs.

Real-World Proof: Made Up, Made Real

The Wright Brothers	Two self-taught bicycle mechanics from Ohio. No aeronautical degrees. No precedence for powered human flight. They made it up, testing wings on sand dunes, crashing, learning, and trying again until they flew.
J.K. Rowling	A single mom scribbling story ideas on napkins in coffee shops. She invented a world from her imagination, and millions have lived in it since.
Steve Jobs and Steve Wozniak	Built the first Apple computer in a garage. No road map. No guarantee. Just an idea, and the willingness to make it up.
Sara Blakely	Founder of Spanx, who took her life savings of $5,000 and cut the feet off her pantyhose in her apartment, creating a multi-billion-dollar company. She said, "I had never taken a business class. I didn't know what I was doing. But I had an idea, and I went for it."
The Founding Fathers	The Constitution of the United States itself is a written invention. There was no global instruction manual for democracy. They made it up, believing in the idea of freedom.

CHAPTER 17

THE ULTIMATE OPERATING SYSTEM

"Now therefore give me this mountain..."
—Caleb, age 85

Throughout this book, we've explored principles of purpose, passion, and vitality in the second half of life. But for many people, there is a deeper motivation—a higher *operating system* guiding every step. That operating system is faith.

Faith is not merely a belief system. It is a way of seeing the world, making decisions, and understanding your purpose on this planet. It is the foundation for your hope, your courage, and your resilience. It reframes every season of life, including the second half, as a season filled not with decline, but divine opportunity.

Approach this chapter not just as a reader, but as a seeker. Inside, you'll find stories that stir the soul—of unshakable perseverance, courageous faith, and vision that defies the odds. Let them challenge you, inspire you, and perhaps most of all, awaken a deeper faith that changes how you see everything. We begin with the story of a spy...

Caleb's Story

He had heard about it his entire life. The promises were passed down from Abraham, Isaac, and Jacob. Tales of a land flowing with milk and honey, of vineyards they hadn't planted, and houses they didn't build. An entire nation was eagerly awaiting this promised freedom after generations of slavery.

Caleb was in his prime when the plagues fell on Egypt. He watched the Nile turn to blood, the skies darken, and the firstborn of Egypt perish. He was there when the Red Sea parted, forming a wall of water on the left and the right, while he and all Israel walked across dry ground.

He tasted manna that fell like dew in the desert, and he followed a pillar of fire at night and a cloud by day. He even heard the voice of God thunder from Mount Sinai. But all of that—the miracles, the memories, the manna—was only a prelude to the real goal: Canaan! The promised land.

After the long and adventurous journey out of Egypt, the moment had finally arrived. And Caleb—strong, faithful, courageous—was honored to be one of the twelve men chosen by Moses to scout out the land. What a mission!

The Spy Expedition

We can envision these twelve spies moving quietly through the hill country, their eyes scanning the terrain and their hearts pounding. It was even better than they imagined. Lush fields and fertile valleys. Grapes so large it took two men to carry a single cluster on a pole. The promise wasn't a myth. It was real and beautiful. But there were other things too—fortified cities, trained warriors, and men so large they seemed inhuman. Giants!

> "Do not go where the path may lead. Go instead where there is no path and leave a trail."
> —Ralph Waldo Emerson

When the twelve spies returned after 40 days, they stood before the people and gave their report. Caleb stepped forward, with confidence showing in his demeanor and voice: *"Let us go up at once and take possession, for we are well able to overcome it"* – Numbers 13:30 (NKV).

But ten of the spies painted a completely different picture. "The land is beautiful," they admitted, "but the people are strong. The cities are fortified. And the giants—oh, the giants!" Those faithless spies ended their speech with a statement that would radically change everything, sending them back into the wilderness for 40 more years:

"There we saw the giants…and we were like grasshoppers in our own sight, and so we were in their sight" – Numbers 13:33 (NKJ).

That one line revealed what was in their hearts all along. But notice that their fear wasn't rooted in fact. It was rooted in identity. They didn't lose the promise because of the giants. They lost it because of their smallness of spirit. They saw themselves as weak, small, and insignificant—and projected that onto their enemies. Never forget the lesson: *What you believe about yourself becomes the reality others perceive.*

If you see yourself as a grasshopper, others will treat you like one. And worse, you'll shrink your dreams down to the size of your fears. But not Caleb.

Faith rarely waits for perfect timing!

He didn't let the shadows define the shape of the future. He saw something bigger, because he served Someone greater.

What made Caleb different? His life was controlled by a higher operating system. Faith! Not a blind hope or a generic spiritual feeling. Faith as an operating system. For both Caleb and Joshua, faith was their internal compass, their fuel, and their lens.

Faith sees what eyes cannot and believes when logic hesitates. It walks forward when others retreat and climbs higher while others settle. Faith doesn't ignore obstacles. It just refuses to be ruled by them.

That's the mindset we need in the second half of life. When the culture says, "You've done enough. Take it easy," faith says: "There's more ahead. Keep going and climb higher." Faith is the lens that redefines how we age, how we dream, and how we finish.

For forty years, Caleb kept himself ready. While others grumbled, he grew. While others declined, he deepened. His body may have aged, but his spirit stayed young. Because faith ages differently. It strengthens in the quiet places and sharpens in delay. Faith matures in the waiting.

A New Chapter Begins

Finally, after 40 long years, they return to the Jordan. This time, however, the river was swollen, raging, and dangerous. It wasn't the ideal moment to cross, but faith rarely waits for perfect timing.

Joshua gives the command. The priests stepped into the floodwaters first, carrying the ark of the covenant—the symbol of God's presence. And as soon as their feet touched the water, the current stopped, while the people followed the marching orders they had received: *"When you see the ark, follow it."*

That's the second-half strategy. Don't follow fear, and don't follow the crowd. Follow the Presence. Step into the water before it parts. This wasn't just a new physical location. It was a new identity, a new mission, a new phase of life. Their second half had begun.

Caleb's Request

And then came Caleb's moment. Now 85 years old, his voice hadn't lost its edge.

> *Here I am this day, eighty-five years old. And yet, I am still as strong this day as on the day that Moses sent me....Now therefore, give me this mountain...*
> — Joshua 14:10-12 (NKJ).

He didn't ask for a quiet valley. He didn't ask for comfort or ease. His request was simple: *I want the land*

God promised me—the one with the giants. He asked for the very place where the giants still lived—the same ones the others had feared all those years ago. He didn't run from the giants. He ran toward them. While others may have looked for comfort, he was looking for a fight. Because when you live by faith, you don't retire, you rise. And your mountain, your calling, doesn't go away just because your age increases.

This isn't just Caleb's story. It's yours. There's a mountain with your name on it. A bold vision. A tough challenge. A deep calling that won't let you go. And you don't have to know all the steps. You just need to take the first one.

When the Fog Rolls In

Earlier in these pages, we reflected on the remarkable Cuba-to-Florida swim—a symbol of persistence and purpose. But long before that courageous crossing, another swimmer faced a different kind of battle. Hers wasn't just a test of distance. It was also a test of vision. And hidden in her story is a timeless truth: sometimes it's not our strength that fails us, but our ability to see beyond the fog.

Her name was Florence Chadwick. She stepped into the waters of the Pacific Ocean off Catalina Island, determined to swim to the shore of California. She had already been the first woman to swim the English Channel both ways. But this day was different. The weather was foggy, and she could hardly see the boats accompanying her. Still, she swam for 15 hours. When she begged to be taken out of the water along the way, her mother, in a boat alongside, told her she was close and could make it. Finally, physically exhausted, she stopped swimming and was pulled out. It wasn't until on the boat that she discovered the shore was less than half a mile away.

At a news conference the next day, she said this: "All I could see was the fog. I think if I could have seen the shore, I would have made it."

That's what faith does. It keeps the shoreline in your soul, even when the fog sets in. It refuses to quit, even when you can't see what's ahead. Florence Chadwick didn't fail because she was weak. She failed because she lost sight of the finish. Two months later, she tried again—same stretch of water, same dense fog—but this time, she kept a mental image of the shoreline in her mind. And she completed the swim with success.

> "We live by faith, not by sight."
> —Paul, Faith Pioneer

That's our call in this season of life. The fog of fear, fatigue, and disappointment will roll in. Giants will still stand in the hills. The river might rage again. But if you keep your eyes on the shoreline—on the promise, the mountain, the calling—you will finish strong.

Faith is the ultimate fuel for a life of never retiring. It is a lens that sees life beyond this life, purpose beyond pleasure, and a legacy that outlives us. It calls us not to retire, but to refire. To view aging not as an end, but as an ascension. A season to multiply wisdom, deepen impact, and prepare to meet the One who gave us breath.

CONCLUSION

Earthrise

*"We shall not cease from exploration,
And the end of all our exploring
Will be to arrive where we started
And know the place for the first time."*
—T.S. Eliot

In the final days of 1968—a year marked by war, unrest, and deep division—three astronauts boarded Apollo 8 and left Earth behind.

Their mission was clear: to orbit the moon and return safely. It was history's first journey to deep space, and every move had been planned down to the second. But the most lasting moment of that mission wasn't in the plan at all.

As their spacecraft emerged from the far side of the moon on the fourth orbit, astronaut Bill Anders looked out the window and saw something no human had ever witnessed: Earth, rising slowly above the lunar horizon. A swirl of blue and white, glowing against the blackness of space.

"We came all this way to explore the Moon, and the most important thing we discovered was the Earth."
—Bill Anders, Apollo 8

He instinctively reached for the camera and captured what would become one of the most iconic photographs in human history: Earthrise.

It was the first time humanity had seen itself from the outside. From 240,000 miles away, our planet looked nothing like the maps we memorize or the headlines we fear. There were no borders, no battle lines, no trace of the noise that fills our days. The distractions faded, and what remained was something sacred: the miracle of life itself.

This is what astronauts now call the *Overview Effect*—a sudden, profound shift in awareness when seeing the planet from space. From above, all boundaries vanish. The Earth looks small, delicate, alive, and united. Astronauts often report a newfound appreciation for the planet's interconnectedness and a profound sense of responsibility toward its preservation.

Apollo 14 astronaut Edgar Mitchell described it like this: *"You develop an instant global consciousness, a people orientation, an intense dissatisfaction with the state of the world, and a compulsion to do something about it."*

A New Perspective. A Greater Finish.

What they experienced in space, you can experience in this stage of life. Above 50, you gain perspective, letting go of trivial annoyances and recognizing your place in the bigger picture. Like astronauts, your vision becomes both broader and sharper.

Conclusion

That single photograph reminds us of something we too easily forget—that we belong to something astonishing. That being alive is a gift, and that perspective changes everything.

This book has challenged the myth of retirement and invited you to a richer story: one of purpose, reinvention, and lifelong contribution. You've encountered people who started again at 50, 60, 70, and above. People who made their greatest impact not despite their age, but because of it. More than anything, you've been reminded of this: you are not finished! You are just getting started. Your life experience—your wisdom, your compassion, your insight—is needed.

As you finish this book, remember that this is where your new chapter begins. Let your presence be a force for good. Let your wisdom be a gift to others. Let your days be filled with purpose—not just for you, but for those who come after you.

Live boldly. Love deeply. And whatever you do...
Never Retire!

ABOUT THE AUTHOR

Bob Loudermilk is a lifelong entrepreneur, inspirational speaker, and founder of the *Never Retire* movement—dedicated to helping people live with purpose, energy, and reinvention in the second half of life.

Bob began his entrepreneurial journey at age 13, when he designed and produced his own neighborhood newspaper, selling copies door-to-door. That early taste of enterprise lit a fire that never went out. His first official business was publishing a marketing magazine for local businesses—followed by a career in corporate training, delivering customized programs in communication, conflict resolution, team building, time management, and sales.

Bob went on to launch *Quantum Expositions*, producing trade shows in multiple U.S. cities, including career fairs and a major entrepreneurship event. For 19 years, he built the company into a respected leader before selling it and relocating to the Oklahoma City area, where his wife had family roots.

Never one to sit still for long, Bob began researching the rapidly growing 50+ demographic and saw an untapped opportunity to help this generation reimagine what's possible. This research became the foundation for the *Second Half Expo*—a widely respected event that connects thousands of adults 50+ with tools, inspiration, and community for thriving in life's next chapter.

Along the way, Bob has invested deeply in mission work, making trips to Russia, South Korea, and most recently, the Philippines, where he shares the Good News, equips leaders, and assists with outreach initiatives. Whether overseas, in a boardroom, or on a conference stage, his passion as an inspirational speaker has remained constant—challenging audiences to step into new possibilities, pursue their higher calling, and live with intentional purpose.

Bob and his wife, Denise, make their home in the Oklahoma City area, where they value time with their children and grandchildren, nurture relationships to encourage others, and enjoy discovering the wider world together through travel.

WHAT'S NEXT?

Your crowning chapter won't happen by accident.
It starts with a single, intentional step. Choose wisely.

If these pages have sparked a desire to go deeper—to keep growing, giving, and making this chapter your boldest and best—here are three powerful ways to move forward:

1. Join Our Community

Join the *Never Retire* movement at: NeverRetire.life
- Exclusive newsletters, email insights, and behind-the-scenes updates.
- Invitations to private online meetups and live Q&A sessions.
- Early access to new resources, tools, and opportunities.

2. Personal Coaching

Work directly with the *Never Retire* team in one-on-one or small-group settings to:
- Identify your passions, strengths, and opportunities.
- Design your second-half blueprint.
- Launch your next chapter with clarity and confidence.

3. For Your Organization

Bring Bob Loudermilk's transformative *Never Retire* keynote to your stage, or collaborate with our experts to craft a workshop experience designed to help your organization:

- Support 50+ employees as they transition into their next purpose-driven chapter.
- Boost engagement, retention, and legacy impact.
- Create a culture that sees age as an asset, not a liability.

Email for Details:
bob@NeverRetire.life

NeverRetire.life

SECOND HALF PRESS

PUBLISHER

Is It Time to Write Your Book?

You have wisdom, experience, and a message worth sharing. But the process of writing and publishing a book can feel overwhelming. Where do you start? How do you finish? And how do you make sure it gets into the hands of readers who need it? That's where we come in.

Second Half Press specializes in helping authors and prospective authors bring their stories and ideas to life. Our professional and dedicated team makes the process clear, simple, and doable—from first draft to finished book.

Why Have a Book?

- A book establishes your authority and credibility.
- A book opens doors—speaking engagements, media features, partnerships.
- A book leaves a legacy for your family, clients, and community.
- A book can become the launchpad for your next chapter of impact.

Why Choose Second Half Press?

- Focused Expertise: We specialize in books written by those in the second half of life—and/or those who serve that audience.
- A Dedicated Team: From editing and design to publishing and promotion, we guide you every step of the way.
- A Simple Process: We take the complexity out of publishing so you can focus on your story and your message.
- A Proven Approach: You'll have a book you'll be confident to share—one that reflects your unique voice, objectives, and vision.

Ready to get started?

If you've dreamed of writing a book, our team makes the process simple, professional, and doable.

Already have a book? Don't let it sit unnoticed. Our marketing team is available to assist with promotional efforts so that you:

- Get your book in front of the right audience
- Build momentum and visibility
- Position yourself as the authority in your field

Email for details:
info@NeverRetire.life

www.ingramcontent.com/pod-product-compliance
Lightning Source LLC
Chambersburg PA
CBHW060144130626
46556CB00006B/2487